D0121398

Law of Torts

UNITED KINGDOM
Sweet & Maxwell Ltd
London

AUSTRALIA
Law Book Co. Ltd.
Sydney

CANADA and USA
Carswell
Toronto

NEW ZEALAND
Brookers
Wellington

SINGAPORE and MALAYSIA
Sweet & Maxwell
Singapore and Kuala Lumpur

Law of Torts

PHILIP BURKE
Griffith College, Dublin

AND

VAL CORBETT
Griffith College, Dublin

DUBLIN
THOMSON ROUND HALL
2003

Published in 2003 by
Round Hall Ltd
43 Fitzwilliam Place
Dublin 2
Ireland

Typeset by
Devlin Editing, Dublin

Printed by
ColourBooks, Dublin

A CIP catalogue record for this book is available from the British Library

ISBN 1-85800-234-6

CONTENTS

TABLE OF CASES

TABLE OF STATUTES

European Union Directives

International Treaties and Conventions

1. AN INTRODUCTION TO THE LAW OF TORTS

1.1 Origin and definition

The word tort is derived from the Latin *tortus*, meaning crooked or twisted. In modern English the term is used as a synonym for "wrong". A tort may be defined as a civil wrong arising from a breach of duty where that duty was imposed not by agreement but by operation of law. Fleming (1998) defines a tort as "an injury other than a breach of contract which the law will redress with damages." While such definitions are helpful to a limited degree, they do not give laypersons any clear conception as to which of their actions may be stigmatised by the courts as tortious, "it does not provide them with a list of the instances where the law allows an injured person the right to recover for his/her injuries" (McMahon & Binchy (2000), p.31). For this reason, we are precluded from providing a comprehensive definition at this point and must be satisfied to adopt a workable description of the concept.

1.2 Torts compared and contrasted with other legal concepts

The tort may be usefully described by comparing and contrasting it with other legal concepts such as criminal and contractual liability. The primary function of the law of torts is to provide a method of redress (in the form of an award of compensatory damages) for individuals who have suffered loss. This function may be contrasted with the object of a criminal prosecution, which is to punish and deter transgressors and to protect society from those who breach the criminal code. However, the compensatory function of the law of torts is not always predominant, as evidenced by those occasions where a judge makes an award of punitive or exemplary damages in a tort action. Such awards are "criminal, vindictive, or punitive in nature" (Salmond & Heuston (1996), p.594) and are therefore out of step with the compensatory nature of the law of torts. A consideration of the academic debate surrounding the legitimacy of awarding such damages will be deferred to our treatment of the law of damages, but it is worth noting at this point that in civil cases the standard of proof is proof on a preponderance or balance of probabilities. This contrasts starkly with the much higher standard of proof applied in criminal matters, *i.e.* proof beyond reasonable doubt, and for this reason the notion of punitive damages rests uneasily within the civil code.

Further overlap exists between the law of torts and the criminal law. For example, a single act of dangerous driving causing injury to a pedestrian constitutes a crime (dangerous driving contrary to section 53 of the Road Traffic Act 1961) whilst also giving rise to liability in tort for the negligent act. In this way we see that one single event may lead to two distinct legal consequences.

The law of torts and contract law are two of the most important areas of the civil law system. A contract is deemed to exist where there has been an agreement between parties, supported by consideration and where the parties intended to create legal relations on foot of their agreement. The contractual relationship is characterised by the concept of privity, which means that only a party to a contract may sue on it. The law of torts operates outside the confines of this doctrine, and therefore a contract is in no way a prerequisite for a successful tort action. The case which best illustrates this fact is *Donoghue v. Stevenson* (1932) where the House of Lords held that a consumer was entitled to recover damages from the manufacturer of a negligently produced product notwithstanding the absence of any contractual relationship between them. In this case, the consumption of the product, a bottle of ginger beer which contained a decomposed snail, caused the plaintiff to suffer gastroenteritis. So it has been succinctly stated that "*Donoghue v. Stevenson* exploded the fallacy that since there was no contract between the plaintiff and the defendant there could be no liability in tort between the parties" (McMahon & Binchy (2000), p.33).

There is also a degree of overlap between the law of torts and contract law. A breach of contract may amount to a tortious act, *e.g.* the selling of a car with faulty brakes. The purchaser of the car who suffers injury whilst driving it may sue for damages for breach of contract but also has the right to recover under tort law on foot of the seller's negligence.

1.3 The fault principle

The fault principle was and, to a lesser degree, remains the cornerstone of the law of torts. However, it should not be presumed that fault is an essential prerequisite for all forms of tortious liability. The tension between strict and fault-based liability in tort law was considered by Oliver Wendell Holmes in *The Path of Law* (1897) where he noted that:

... the traditional policy of our law is to confine liability to cases where a prudent man might have foreseen the injury or at least the danger, while the inclination of a very large part of the community is to make certain classes of persons insure the safety of those with whom they deal.

Indeed, in those areas of the law of torts which are considered to be in greatest need of reform, the proposals for change such as those contained in the Pearson Committee Report 1978 almost inevitably involve the substitution of strict for fault-based liability. The imposition of strict liability allows for the recovery of damages against a defendant on a "no fault" basis. In the words of Winfield & Jolowicz (2002), p. 28:

Since the law of tort is a system of establishing *liability* it is obvious that it could never have compensated all victims of misfortune. At the very least there must be some causal link between an activity of the defendant and the injury to the plaintiff. There is, however, no logically compelling reason why the law should have chosen fault as the determinant of this liability (emphasis added).

This significant move towards strict liability is most pronounced in areas such as product liability (under The Liability for Defective Products Act 1991) and liability for failure to control animals (for example, section 21(1) of the Control of Dogs Acts 1986–1992). However, the imposition of no-fault liability should not be considered to be a modern innovation, as evidenced by the long-established rule in *Rylands v. Fletcher* (1868) concerning liability for the escape of dangerous things:

Despite the continuing dominance of fault liability the law of tort does contain certain limited principles of strict liability with regard to personal injuries. Some of these are of common law origin and of respectable antiquity, others have been the creation of modern statutes and have either been limited in their practical importance or are of rather haphazard application. It is unlikely that any consistent policy has been followed in the creation of these areas of strict liability, though it is perhaps possible to discern behind them some very hazy idea of unusual or increased risk (Winfield & Jolowicz (2002), pp. 35–36).

2. NEGLIGENCE

2.1 Introduction

Negligence is both a specific tort and a mode of committing other torts, and may be described as the failure to exercise that care which a reasonable man would exercise in all the circumstances of the case. Therefore, negligence may consist of omitting to do something which ought to be done, or doing something which ought to be done either in a different manner or not at all. In a similar vein, in *Blyth v. Birmingham Waterworks* (1856), Alderson B. stated:

> Negligence is the omission to do something which a reasonable man, guided upon those considerations which ordinarily regulate the conduct of human affairs, would do, or doing something which a prudent and reasonable man would not do.

The tort of negligence has a relatively recent origin, but is undoubtedly the most broad based of all torts. The modern tort of negligence is founded on the neighbour principle developed by Lord Atkin in *Donoghue v. Stevenson* (1932). Prior to 1932, the law had been built up in disconnected slabs exhibiting a complete lack of unity of structure. Instead of one unified concept of duty of care, there were over 50 separate duties of care recognised. Negligence was not regarded as a tort in its own right until the late nineteenth century. However, early case law did suggest that in certain situations liability based on carelessness could arise. From earliest times, it was recognised that innkeepers and common carriers could be liable for the careless performance of their tasks. In the seventeenth century, it was established that a surgeon or an attorney would be liable for conduct which was less than that expected of a reasonably skilled professional. Fleming (1998, p.113) notes that

> what slender notion there was about negligence, developed in connection with the amorphous action on the case, but until the 19th century this yielded little more than "a bundle of frayed ends".

Lord Atkin's formulation of the concept of "neighbourhood" as a means for determining the existence of a duty of care provided the impetus for the remarkable development of the modern tort of negligence.

2.2 Elements of negligence

The tort of negligence consists of three essential elements, the duty of care, breach of that duty by the defendant and damage resulting from the breach.

2.2.1 Duty of care

The concept of duty determines whether the type of loss suffered by the plaintiff is, in all the circumstances of the case, actionable. The duty of care, if it is held to exist, is owed only to those persons who are in the area of foreseeable danger.

2.2.2 Breach of duty

Breach of duty is concerned with the standard of care that ought to have been reached by the defendant, in all the circumstances of the case, to avoid liability in negligence. An objective standard is applied and the defendant's conduct is judged against the standard of the "reasonable man." It is no defence for a party to establish that, in connection with the impugned course of conduct, he did his best to avoid causing the plaintiff loss if his best fell below the standard that would have been met by a reasonable man.

2.2.3 Damage

Finally, damage must have been suffered by the plaintiff as a result of the defendant's breach of duty. The tort of negligence is not complete until the plaintiff has suffered some actionable damage, injury or loss which would be capable of attracting an award of compensation or damages in a court of law.

3. NEGLIGENCE: THE DUTY OF CARE

3.1 Introduction

The common law narrows the field of potential litigants in any action based in negligence to those who can establish that they were owed a duty of care. There must be, in the words of Lord Atkin in *Donoghue v. Stevenson* (1932), "some general conception of relations giving rise to a duty of care" between the parties. The existence of such a duty may be obvious in the majority of cases, *e.g.* pedestrian/motorist, doctor/patient etc. However, in some cases the relationship may not be as readily identifiable and in such circumstances the question of a duty arising may, as Quill (1999, p.21) points out "raise complex questions of public policy which require value judgements to determine which competing interest should attract greater protection under the law."

3.2 Establishment of the duty of care: the neighbour principle

The modern tort of negligence originated with the House of Lords' decision in *Donoghue v. Stevenson* (1932). In that case, the plaintiff consumed a bottle of ginger beer purchased for her by a friend. The ginger beer was contained in a dark bottle opened on her behalf by the café owner. The plaintiff drank some of the beer and as she poured the remainder into her glass, the remains of a decomposed snail fell out of the bottle. The plaintiff became ill and brought an action in negligence against the manufacturer of the drink. The plaintiff argued that the manufacturer of the ginger beer owed her a duty of care not to produce the beer negligently, particularly in a situation where the form in which it left the manufacturer (in a sealed bottle) was the form it was intended to reach the ultimate consumer. While the case is important as a watershed in product liability law, it is probably more famous because of Lord Atkin's neighbour principle in which he set out the framework for determining the existence of a duty of care:

> The rule that you are to love your neighbour becomes in law you must not injure your neighbour; and the lawyer's question who is my neighbour? receives a restricted reply. You must take reasonable care to avoid acts or omissions which you can reasonably foresee would be

liable to injure your neighbour. Who, then, in law, is my neighbour? The answer seems to be – persons who are so closely and directly affected by my act that I ought reasonably to have them in contemplation as being so affected when I am directing my mind to the acts or omissions which are called in question.

It is evident from even a summary examination of Lord Atkin's statement that the central element in establishing the existence of a legal duty to take care is the relationship between the parties concerned. Under Lord Atkin's formula, if the parties were considered in the eyes of the law to be "neighbours", then a duty of care may arise.

The question which must then be asked is, who is one's neighbour? In order to determine whether a legal relationship of neighbourhood exists, the court will consider whether the defendant could reasonably foresee that the plaintiff (who is in a proximate relationship with the defendant) would have been so injured if the defendant were to act carelessly in relation to him.

3.3 The foreseeable plaintiff

The plaintiff must be the foreseeable victim of the defendant's actions. The "law does not recognise a duty in the air" (*per* Greer L.J. in *Bottomley v. Bannister* (1932)), and liability will not rest with the defendant where he could not have reasonably contemplated injury occurring to the plaintiff. A demonstration of this particular aspect of the duty of care is found in the case of *Palsgraf v. Long Island Rail Road* (1928), where employees of the defendant company negligently caused a parcel to be knocked from a passenger's grasp as he was boarding a train. Unbeknownst to the defendant's employees, the parcel contained fireworks, which were set off, causing a minor explosion. The resultant vibrations allegedly caused scales some distance down the platform to fall over and strike the plaintiff. It was held that while the defendants did certainly owe a duty of care to the passenger boarding the train and were liable for the damage caused to him, the plaintiff could not succeed in her action. She was, in the eyes of the law, a totally unforeseeable victim of the defendant's negligence as she was some distance from the negligent act. Cardozo J. delivered the majority opinion of the court and explained the decision in the following words:

A wrong to another cannot be the basis of the plaintiff's claim and even less a wrong to a mere property interest ... The victim does not sue derivatively or by right of subrogation to vindicate an interest in the person of another ... He sues for breach of duty owed to himself.

Similar reasoning was adopted in the English case of *Bourhill v. Young* (1943). In that case, a man was killed in a motorcycle accident. The plaintiff was standing some distance away when the collision occurred. She claimed that the sound of the collision and sight of its aftermath caused her to have a miscarriage and suffer from nervous shock. The defendant was not found to be liable to the plaintiff in the circumstances. The Court held that she was an unforeseeable victim of the defendant's negligence. In rejecting the plaintiff's claim, Lord Wright adopted the reasoning of Cardozo J. in *Palsgraf*, stating that the plaintiff could not "build upon a wrong to someone else."

The decisions in *Palsgraf* and *Bourhill* highlight the divergence between altruism and common law negligence. While both plaintiffs may have been blameless for their injuries, the courts did not recompense them. While the law of negligence is not concerned with compensating all those injured as a result of the defendant's act, a more altruistic view would hold that the defendant should be liable for all the consequences of his negligent actions that cause injury to another. This noble point of view was put forward in the dissenting opinion of Andrews J. in *Palsgraf*, when he said that:

> Everyone owes to the world at large a duty of refraining from those acts which unreasonably threaten the safety of others .... When there is an unreasonable act and some right that may be affected there is negligence ... It is a wrong not only to those who happen to be within the radius of danger but to all who might have been there.

However, the law of negligence is not motivated by unselfishness. Practical and policy factors must be taken into consideration. The consequences of recognising the existence of liability in the manner outlined by Andrews J. would be too drastic and would in certain situations place an intolerable (and perhaps unfair) burden on the shoulders of the negligent defendant.

3.4 Development of negligence: the English approach

One of the unique characteristics of the duty of care framework is its ability to allow the tort of negligence to develop to meet novel factual situations. Following *Donoghue*, it was no longer necessary "to bring the facts of [a] situation within those of previous situations in which a duty of care ha[d] been held to exist" (*per* Lord Wilberforce in *Anns v.*

Merton London Borough Council (1978)). In the years following *Donoghue,* the limits of negligence continued to expand. In *Hedley Byrne v. Heller* (1964), the court imposed a duty of care in cases involving economic loss where, hitherto no duty was found to exist. Similarly, in *Dorset Yacht Co. Ltd v. Home Office* (1970), the Crown was found liable in negligence to the plaintiff where juveniles who had escaped from a local penal institution damaged its boat.

In light of these developments, Lord Wilberforce in *Anns v. Merton London Borough Council* (1978) attempted to refine the neighbour principle. Under Lord Wilberforce's formulation, the plaintiff was required to satisfy a two-stage test before the existence of a duty of care could be established:

> First, one has to ask whether, as between the alleged wrongdoer and the person who has suffered damage, there is a sufficient relationship of proximity or neighbourhood such that, in the reasonable contemplation of the former, carelessness on his part may be likely to cause damage to the latter, in which case a prima facie duty of care arises. Secondly, if the first question is to be answered affirmatively, it is necessary to consider whether there are any considerations which ought to negative, or to reduce or limit the scope of, the duty or the class of person to whom it is owed or the damages to which a breach of it may rise ....

Whether intentional or not, Lord Wilberforce's refinement of the neighbour principle in *Anns* led to a subtle, yet substantial shift in judicial attitude in Britain. Subsequent judgments in cases such as *McLoughlin v. O'Brian* (1983) and *Junior Books v. Veitchi Co. Ltd* (1982) approved the decision and interpreted the two-step test in an expansionist manner. Under this interpretation, if the plaintiff could establish that it was reasonably foreseeable that the defendant's carelessness was likely to cause damage to him, then a relationship of proximity would be found to exist between the parties and a *prima facie* duty of care would arise. The existence of a presumption of a duty of care could only then be rebutted by public policy considerations.

The English judiciary's interpretation of *Anns* widens the scope of the duty of care. In the view of many – initially at least – Lord Wilberforce's test represented the true spirit of *Donoghue v. Stevenson,* as it provided a framework in which the tort could continue to develop. However, the judgment was not without its critics. In *Governors of the Peabody Donation Fund v. Sir Lindsay Parkinson & Co. Ltd* (1985) and in *Leigh and Sullivan Ltd v. Aliakmon Shipping Co. Ltd* (1986), the first soundings of the death knell for the principle were heard, with

Lord Brandon stating in the latter case that *Anns* did not provide "a universally applicable test of the existence and scope of a duty of care in the law of negligence."

One of the central criticisms of the liberal interpretation of Lord Wilberforce's exposition of the duty of care principle was that it made it far too easy for a plaintiff to establish the existence of a duty of care. Liability would be presumed where, based on the circumstances, the defendant should have foreseen injury to the plaintiff. This view indicated an over-reliance on the concept of reasonable foreseeability (unqualified by other factors such as proximity) in recognising a duty of care, and as "almost everything in life is foreseeable if you have a vivid enough imagination" (Mullis & Oliphant, (1997), p. 21), it was an undemanding barrier for a plaintiff to negotiate. In practice, the policy factors were only used in exceptional circumstances to rebut a finding of a duty of care. As a result, the two-stage test in *Anns* led to the liberalisation of the law of negligence in the following years, leading ultimately to the case of *Junior Books v. Veitchi Co. Ltd* (1982), where a duty of care was found to exist between the the defendant, who was engaged to install a factory floor, and the owner of the factory, notwithstanding the fact that the installers' negligence had only caused economic loss to the plaintiff.

The misgivings expressed by the judiciary in *Peabody* and *Leigh* were echoed in *Yuen Kun-yeu v. A.G. of Hong Kong* (1987), where the Privy Council warned of the dangers of equating proximity with reasonable foreseeability when determining the existence of a duty of care:

> Foreseeability of harm is a necessary ingredient of such a relationship, but it is not the only one. Otherwise there would be liability in negligence on the part of one who sees another about to walk over a cliff with his head in the air, and forbears to shout a warning.

The death-knell for Lord Wilberforce's formula, under English law at least, came with the House of Lords' decision in *Caparo Industries v. Dickman* (1990), rejecting the liberal interpretation of *Anns*. It was held that negligence law should no longer be developed in such an unrestrained manner where a duty of care could be recognised in every case based on general principle and without regard to other cases. Rather, in what has been described as the "incremental approach," it was felt that the tort should develop on a case-by-case basis akin to the historical approach of placing cases into specific categories. Lord Bridge stated:

[I]n addition to the foreseeability of damage, necessary ingredients in any situation giving rise to a duty of care are that there should exist between the party owing the duty and the party to whom it is owed a relationship characterised by the law as one of "proximity" or "neighbourhood" and that the situation should be one in which the court considers fair, just and reasonable that the law should impose a duty of a given scope on the one party for the benefit of the other.

Under Lord Bridge's approach, the concepts of "reasonable foreseeability" and "proximity" were split, thereby creating separate and distinct hurdles which were to be negotiated by the plaintiff. Having satisfied the twin tests of reasonable foreseeability and proximity, the court would then decide whether it considered that it would be fair, just and reasonable to impose a duty of care in that particular situation. With regard to the concepts of proximity, justice and reasonableness, Lord Bridge expressed the view that these concepts were indefinable and mere convenient labels to attach to the features of different specific situations. Crucially, it was his Lordship's view that the theme underlying these "criteria" was one of incremental development to which the other "criteria" were subservient.

Lord Bridge's words were a reflection of how the tide had turned against the *Anns* principle, in favour of a more conservative and incremental approach. The separation of the concepts of reasonable foreseeability and proximity ensure that a finding of a duty of care did not become the formality it had become following *Anns* and *Junior Books*. Furthermore, even in situations where both the foreseeability and proximity questions produced affirmative answers, a duty of care would not be recognised unless it was just and reasonable to do so (*Caparo*).

The importance of public policy considerations under the *Caparo* test should not be underestimated. A duty of care, notwithstanding the existence of proximity and reasonable foreseeability, will not be recognised by the court where it is of the opinion that it would be against the interests of society as a whole to recognise such a duty. A duty may not be recognised in such circumstances where the court is of the opinion that the establishment of the duty will open the "floodgates" (a flood of similar actions) or will overburden the defendant with excessive liability. While the law of negligence should encourage greater care between persons, it should not give rise to over-caution. In *Hill v. Chief Constable of West Yorkshire* (1989), the plaintiffs brought an action in negligence against the defendant. The plaintiff's daughter had been the final victim of the "Yorkshire Ripper", Peter Sutcliffe. The plaintiff alleged that the defendant's negligence in the investigation of Sutcliffe's crimes led to her daughter's murder. The House of Lords dismissed the plaintiff's appeal. Lord Templeman explained that the imposition of liability in the circumstances would do more harm than good and on public policy grounds, an action could not lie:

> ... if this action lies, every citizen will be able to require the court to investigate the performance of every policeman. If the policeman concentrates on one crime, he may be accused of neglecting others. The threat of litigation against a police force would not make a policeman more efficient. The necessity for defending proceedings successfully or unsuccessfully, would distract the policeman from his duties.

The decision in *Hill* effectively granted the police immunity from a prosecution in negligence regarding the conduct of their investigations, and was challenged as violating the citizen's right of access to the courts under the European Convention on Human Rights (which had been incorporated into English law in 1998), in *Osman v. United Kingdom* (1999). In that case, the European Court found that the House of Lords' decision in *Hill* created blanket immunity in favour of the police and amounted to an unjustifiable restriction on the applicant's right to have a determination on the merits of his or her case. The decision could have had far reaching implications for the law of negligence as it applied in the U.K. However, the European Court of Human Rights retreated from this position in its later decision in *Z v. U.K.*, where the court appeared to admit that its decision in *Osman* may have been based on a misapprehension of English domestic law:

> The Court considers that its reasoning in the *Osman* judgement was based on an understanding of the law of negligence ... which has to be reviewed in the light of the clarifications subsequently made by the domestic courts and notably the House of Lords ... In the present case, the Court is led to the conclusion that the inability of the applicants to sue the local authority flowed not from an immunity but from the applicable principles governing the substantive right of action in domestic law.

The potential of the decision in *Osman* to dismantle the negligence framework erected in *Caparo* did not materialise following the decision in *Z v. U.K.* However, the decision in *Osman* is further evidence, if any was required, of the Byzantine nature and role of public policy in common law judicial decision-making and the difficulties created by them when attempting to establish the existence of a duty of care in any given situation.

3.5 Development of negligence: the Irish approach

The neighbour principle as outlined in *Donoghue* was endorsed by Gavan Duffy J. in the Irish case of *Kirby v. Burke & Holloway* (1944). However, the Irish and English jurisdictions have diverged in their interpretation of Lord Wilberforce's judgment in *Anns*. Whereas their English counterparts were of the view that *Anns* was the cue for the expansion of the tort, the Irish judiciary merely saw the case as a reiteration of the neighbour principle (albeit worded differently) laid down by Lord Atkin. The stance taken by the Irish courts was articulated by Costello P. in *H.M.W. v. Ireland* (1997) as follows:

> The view of the Irish courts has been that *Anns* was a "confirmation" of the long established principles of the law of tort contained in *Donoghue v. Stevenson* and was not (as some commentators in England seem to consider) a major innovation in the law of tort.

The opposing views adopted by the Irish and English judiciary to the decision in *Anns* led to differing approaches to duty of care being taken by each jurisdiction. The view initially adopted under English law equated the principle of foreseeability with proximity. The key difference in the Irish approach was the placing of increased reliance on the concept of proximity as a tool for establishing the existence of a duty of care.

The requirement of proximity is important in that it provides a check on the test of reasonable foreseeability. Reasonable foreseeability alone as a test for determining the duty of care would be insufficient. Take, for example, the passer-by who witnesses a young child playing near a duck pond. It is reasonably foreseeable that this child may fall into the pond and drown. However, the law will not impose a duty of care on the passer-by for omitting to stop the child from drowning. There is no legally proximate relationship between the child and the passer-by such as would justify the imposition of an obligation on the passer-by to ensure that the child does not come to harm. However, if the child in question is on a school trip, the school will be held to owe a duty of care to that child in the circumstances. The danger to the child is reasonably foreseeable *and* there is a proximate relationship between the schoolteachers and the child, *i.e.* the child has been entrusted to their supervision.

Proximity in this context is difficult to define. As McMahon & Binchy (2000, pp. 119-120) have opined, the word:

... suggests a closeness between the parties, but on analysis it turns out that the legal notion of proximity does not require closeness in either space or time. Liability in negligence may attach to conduct that results in injury or damage thousands of miles away and decades later to a plaintiff not born at the time when the conduct was completed. It is true that distance in space and time are factors to which due weight is to be given when deciding the question of legal proximity, but these factors are far from the only ones.

The importance placed on the concept of proximity in Irish negligence law was evident from the decision of McCarthy J. in the Supreme Court case of *Ward v. McMaster* (1988). In that case, the plaintiffs purchased a house with the assistance of a loan from their local authority. The local authority commissioned a survey of the house which was carried out negligently and which failed to disclose the existence of a number of structural defects, both dangerous and non-dangerous. The plaintiffs sued both the builder/vendor and the local authority. The plaintiffs argued that the local authority should have been aware that they were lacking in means and could not afford to commission their own survey of the property and therefore were relying on the survey commissioned by the local authority (which was carried out negligently). On appeal, the Supreme Court found that the local authority did indeed owe the plaintiffs a duty of care, notwithstanding the fact that the loss in question could be labelled as purely economic. McCarthy J. in his judgment in the case approved the test espoused by Lord Wilberforce in *Anns*, stating:

> ... I prefer to express the duty as arising from the proximity of the parties, the foreseeability of the damage, and the absence of any compelling exemption based on public policy, I do not, in any fashion, seek to exclude the latter consideration, although I confess that such a consideration must be a very powerful one if it is to be used to deny an injured party his right to redress at the expense of the person or body that injured him.

McCarthy J. in the above passage appeared to lay down a three-step approach towards the duty of care issue. First, a plaintiff must establish a proximate relationship between the parties. Second, the damage must be foreseeable. Third, there must be no convincing policy reasons why a duty should not be recognised.

McCarthy J. expressly rejected the incremental approach favoured under English law following *Caparo,* stating that the "verbally attractive proposition of incremental growth ... suffers from a temporal defect – that rights should be determined by the accident of birth." The incremental approach expanded the boundaries of the duty of care on a case-by-case basis with reference to similar preceding cases. The liberal view championed by McCarthy J. would allow the tort to leap forward meeting the requirements of "new" factual situations based more on the concepts of reasonable foreseeability and proximity than judicial precedent. The valid criticism made by McCarthy J. of the incremental approach highlights the fact that whether a duty of care exists in a particular situation would greatly depend on the timing of the circumstances giving rise to a claim. If it should occur at a time when an analogous case has not yet come before the courts, then the plaintiff may face an uphill struggle to establish a duty of care. Alternatively, if the action is brought at a time where similar cases have already recognised a duty of care, then it may prove much easier to establish such a duty.

The test expounded by McCarthy J. in *Ward* was very different to that put forward under English Law immediately following *Anns*. The test laid down in *Ward*, despite its rejection of the incremental approach, was sterner than that initially adopted in English law. A duty of care would only be found to exist where the twin tests of reasonable foreseeability and proximity were satisfied, policy only intervening where there were strong reasons for doing so.

3.5.1 Glencar Exploration v. Mayo County Council *(2001)*: Ireland's retrenchment from *Anns?*

The recent Supreme Court judgment of Keane C.J. in *Glencar Exploration v. Mayo County Council* (2001) involves a retreat from the views expressed by McCarthy J. in *Ward*. In *Glencar*, the applicant was a mining company that had been granted renewable mining licences for the County Mayo region by the Minister for Energy in 1968. The respondent introduced a mining ban as part of its development plan in 1992, despite the fact that the applicant had up to that time invested heavily in undertaking prospecting activities in the area. It was also alleged that a lucrative joint venture arrangement entered into by the applicant with another company collapsed as a direct result of the imposition of the mining ban. The applicant initiated proceedings seeking a declaration that the administrative action of introducing the ban was *ultra vires*, and claimed damages for negligence and breach of duty. In his judgment, Keane C.J., in refusing the applicant relief, highlighted the difficulties that these concepts had posed for the courts, noting that the concept of reasonable foreseeability "was a necessary but, of itself, insufficient condition of liability in negligence."

Keane C.J. questioned the conventional wisdom which held that *Ward v. McMaster* represented an unqualified approval of the two-stage test in *Anns,* arguing that it was "by no means clear" from the judgments that this was so. Keane C.J. went so far as to question whether the observations of McCarthy J. in *Ward* formed part of the *ratio* of that decision. He commented that:

> Given the far reaching implications of adopting in this jurisdiction a principle of liability in negligence from which there has been such powerful dissent in other common law jurisdictions, I would not be prepared to hold that further consideration of the underlying principles is foreclosed by the dicta of McCarthy J. in *Ward v. McMaster.*

In perhaps the most illuminating part of the judgment, the Chief Justice expressly approved of the conservative approach taken by the English judiciary in decisions such as *Caparo*:

> There is, in my view, no reason why courts determining whether a duty of care arises should consider themselves obliged to hold that it does in every case where injury or damage to property was reasonably foreseeable and the notoriously difficult and elusive test of "proximity" or neighbourhood" can be said to have been met, unless very powerful public policy considerations dictate otherwise. It seems to me that no injustice will be done if they are required to take the further step of considering whether, in all the circumstances, it is just and reasonable that the law should impose a duty of given scope on the defendant for the benefit of the plaintiff, as held by Costello J. at first instance in *Ward v. McMaster,* by Brennan J. in *Sutherland Shire Council v. Heyman* and by the House of Lords in *Caparo Industries Plc. v. Dickman.* As Brennan J. pointed out, there is a significant risk that any other approach will result in what he called a "massive extension of a *prima facie* duty of care restrained only by undefinable considerations ..."

These words signify an important shift in Irish judicial thinking regarding the duty of care concept, representing a move towards the incremental approach that has formed the basis for English judicial thinking since *Caparo.* Further guidance as to when it may be "just and reasonable" to impose a duty of care can be found in the judgment of Brennan J. in the High Court of Australia in *Sutherland Shire Council v. Heyman* (1985), where he stated that:

> It is preferable in my view, that the law should develop novel categories of negligence incrementally and by analogy with established categories, rather than by a massive extension of a *prima facie* duty of care restrained only be indefinable "considerations which ought to

negative, or to reduce or limit the scope of the duty or the class of person to whom it is owed".

It is submitted that the judgment of Keane C.J. has for the first time since *Anns*, reunited the English and Irish judiciaries in their attitude towards the duty of care. The judgment of the Chief Justice involves the placing of particular emphasis on the concepts of justice and reasonableness, whilst reiterating the distinct identity of the notions of reasonable foreseeability and proximity. Further, public policy considerations are essentially sidelined in favour of the pursuit of a precedent where a duty has been held to exist in analogous circumstances.

It may be too early to state the precise implications of the Supreme Court's judgment in *Glencar*. However, it is submitted that this apparent move towards incrementalism will not have the same dramatic effect as it did in England following *Caparo* and *Murphy*. In Ireland, *Anns*, while liberally interpreted, always involved a clear identification of the separate concepts of proximity and foreseeability, ensuring that a finding of duty never became a formality. The English judiciary's interpretation of *Anns*, created something akin to a presumption of the existence of the duty of care in all but the most exceptional of cases and as such, the move towards incrementalism effected a much more dramatic change in the legal landscape.

4. NEGLIGENCE: THE DUTY OF CARE – SPECIAL SITUATIONS

4.1 Introduction

The concept of duty of care is primarily concerned with identifying the class of persons to whom the defendant may be liable in negligence. However, it is important to remember that the duty question is also relevant to the kind of harm that may provide the plaintiff with a cause of action in negligence. Thus, in areas such as pure economic loss and liability for psychiatric damage, the existence of a duty of care may be denied, notwithstanding the fact that the orthodox test of neighbourhood has been satisfied, because of the courts' reticence to recognise a duty in connection with this type of harm.

4.2 Economic loss

Financial loss arising as a direct consequence of physical damage negligently caused by the defendant is recoverable in tort and is known as consequential economic loss. For example, if a plaintiff's car is negligently damaged, he is entitled to compensation for the economic loss he has incurred as a consequence of the physical damage suffered. However, damage which is purely financial in nature and is unaccompanied by any physical damage has traditionally been treated differently by the courts. The courts have been reluctant to award compensation for pure economic loss on policy grounds. The possibility of an indeterminate number of claims arising from one incidence of negligence (the floodgates argument) is one reason why compensation for such damage is awarded only in exceptional circumstances. The possible knock-on effects of recognising liability for causing such damage would unduly burden the defendants. As Lord Pearce observed in *Hedley Byrne & Co. v. Heller & Partners Ltd* (1964):

> Economic protection has lagged behind protection in physical matters where there is injury to person and property. It may be that the size and the width of the range of possible claims has acted as a deterrent to extension of economic protection.

In *Cattle v. Stockton Waterworks Co.* (1875), the plaintiff was contracted to build a tunnel on property belonging to a third party. As a result of the defendant's negligence, a water pipe burst, making the building of the tunnel much more expensive for the plaintiff. The plaintiff sued in negligence for the extra expense he had incurred. His claim in negligence was dismissed on the ground that this type of injury was not foreseeable and a finding for the plaintiff in this context could potentially create indeterminate liability. The case of *Spartan Steel and Alloys Ltd v. Martin & Co. Ltd* (1973) provides another instructive example of the courts' attitude towards compensation for pecuniary loss unaccompanied by physical damage. In that case, the defendant builders were carrying out work close to the plaintiff's steel factory. The defendant negligently damaged an electricity cable leading to the factory and as a result, power to the factory was cut off for a number of hours. The plaintiff sued for the loss of profits that it had suffered while the factory was not in operation. The plaintiff succeeded in recovering damages for the steel that was damaged as a result of the power shortage as this loss was a consequence of the defendants' negligence. However, the plaintiff did not succeed in its claim in relation to the steel they *could have* manufactured but for the negligence of the defendant. This damage was not recoverable, as it was purely economic in nature. Lord Denning explained the different approach taken by the courts towards claims for compensation of a purely financial nature, stating, "if claims for economic loss were permitted for this particular hazard there would be no end of claims. Some might be genuine, but many might be inflated or even false."

4.2.1 Economic loss caused by negligent misstatements

Notwithstanding the general tendency of the courts to deny recovery for purely economic loss, there are a number of important exceptions. Pure economic loss may be recoverable under tort law where such loss is caused by a negligent statement made by one party to another, if that statement is made in a situation where, based on the special relationship between the parties, it is reasonably foreseeable that that other will rely on the statement. In that situation, the maker of the statement will be liable where the recipient relies on the advice to his detriment.

Liability for negligent misstatements was established in England by the House of Lords' decision in *Hedley Byrne & Co. Ltd v. Heller & Partners Ltd* (1964). In that case, the plaintiff entered into business relations with another company called Easipower Ltd As a result of this relationship, the plaintiff became personally liable under a number of contractual agreements and they requested a credit reference from Easipower Ltd's bank. The defendant bank replied in a letter stating that the advice given was for the defendant's "private use and without responsibility on the part of the bank or its officials." The letter confirmed that Easipower Ltd was in a sound financial position. Soon after, Easipower Ltd went into liquidation and the plaintiff suffered financial loss as a result. The House of Lords held that the defendant was absolved from responsibility for the negligent advice because of the disclaimer contained within the letter. However, the decision has particular importance as the House of Lords recognised for the first time that there could be recovery for pure economic loss in such circumstances. Lord Morris observed that:

> It should now be regarded as settled that if someone possessed of a special skill undertakes, quite irrespective of contract, to apply that skill for the assistance of another person who relies upon that skill, a duty of care will arise ... Furthermore, if, in a sphere in which a person is so placed that others could reasonably rely upon his judgement or his skill or upon his ability to make careful inquiry, a person takes it upon himself to give information or advice to, or allows his information or advice to be passed on to, another person who, as he knows or should know, will place reliance upon it, then a duty of care will arise.

Lord Reid stated that any reasonable man, knowing his skill and judgement were being relied upon, would have a number of options open to him. First, he could keep silent and not give any advice or make any statement. Second, he could give an answer, but qualify it as being made without responsibility (as occurred in *Hedley Byrne*). Third, he could give an answer without any such qualification. In the first two scenarios, the maker of the statement would not be liable for any loss caused to another as a result of reliance on the advice. However, where he took the last course of action and gave such advice without any qualification, then he must, according to Lord Reid, "be held to have accepted some responsibility for his answer being given carefully, or to have accepted a relationship with the inquirer which requires him to exercise such care as the circumstances require."

The decision of the House of Lords in *Hedley Byrne* was endorsed by the Irish High Court in *Securities Trust Ltd v. Hugh Moore Alexander Ltd* (1964). In that case, the Articles of Association of the defendant company were negligently misprinted. The misprinted articles were then forwarded to a shareholder upon his request. The shareholder, who was also the managing director of the plaintiff company, caused the plaintiff company to invest in the defendant's shares and the plaintiff incurred substantial financial losses as a result. It was held on the facts of the particular case that the defendant company did not owe the plaintiff company a duty of care as the error was communicated to the plaintiff's managing director in his role as a shareholder. As result, the plaintiff was not the intended recipient of the information.

The maker of a negligent statement does not owe a duty to the world at large in respect of the statement made, and in *Bank of Ireland v. Smith* (1966), the Irish courts emphasised that the existence of a "special relationship" was central to the establishment of a duty of care. In that case, an auctioneer incorrectly stated in an advertisement that certain land was in pasture. Relying on the statement, the plaintiff purchased the land. The court found that the auctioneer did not owe the plaintiff a duty of care regarding the misleading statement, since no special relationship existed between the auctioneer and the purchaser, the auctioneer's primary duty being owed to the vendor and not the plaintiff. This decision may be contrasted with the High Court's decision in *McCullagh v. PB Gunne* (1997), where an auctioneer, an employee of the defendant, proactively assisted a couple in the purchase of licensed premises. He promised the couple that he would arrange the finance for the purchase and told them that he had not advertised the sale to the general public since he feared a deluge of enquiries. In fact, his reason for not advertising the property was that the vendor had requested him to keep the sale as private as possible. Prior to purchase, he also advised the plaintiffs that should the premises be resold they would make a profit in the region of £10,000 to £20,000. In her judgment, Carroll J. noted that an auctioneer's first duty was to the client (the vendor) and that "auctioneers cannot be all things to all men." However, in this case the auctioneer, based on his close involvement with the couple, could foresee that they would rely on his advice and in such circumstances he was found to owe a duty of care to them. A special relationship was also found to exist in *Smith v. Eric S Bush* (1990), where a surveyor employed to value a house for a financial institution in order to determine whether it was adequate security for a mortgage was found to be liable both to the financial institution and the mortgagee, where the valuation was carried out negligently.

Foreseeability of reliance is critical to a successful action for negligent misstatement. In *Gayson v. Allied Irish Banks plc* (2000), the plaintiff was a customer of the defendant bank and the holder of an off-shore bank account. He alleged that he had been negligently advised by the defendant's employee not to avail of the 1988 tax amnesty. Geoghegan J. found that the conversation between the bank official and the plaintiff was very informal and "off the cuff" and therefore neither party could have foreseen that the plaintiff would have relied on the information as he did thereby giving rise to an action for negligent misstatement.

As in all cases of negligence, the plaintiff must establish that the damage he has suffered in reliance on the statement was reasonably foreseeable. In *Reeman v. Department of Transport* (1997), the plaintiff relied on a certificate of seaworthiness issued by the defendant when purchasing a vessel. The certificate was negligently issued and the plaintiff incurred considerable financial expense in having defects in the boat repaired. The plaintiff's action for negligent misstatement failed, as the plaintiff did not establish the requisite proximity between the parties since the certificate was produced as evidence of safety, and not for commercial purposes. In *Morgan Crucible Co. v. Hill Samuel Bank* (1991), an accountant was held to owe a duty to a takeover bidder in circumstances where he gave negligent advice in the form of a specially prepared audit that the bidder had relied upon. The completion of the special audit created the necessary degree of proximity to ground a successful action. Conversely, in *Caparo Industries plc v. Dickman* (1990) the plaintiff, relying on the statutorily prepared accounts of the company, tabled a takeover bid. The accounts had been negligently prepared and showed a profit instead of a loss. As a result of its reliance, the plaintiff suffered heavy financial losses. The plaintiff's action for negligent misstatement was unsuccessful. The accounts were not specifically prepared with the plaintiff's purpose in mind, and the necessary degree of proximity was absent. Lord Jauncey observed that:

> If the statutory accounts are prepared and distributed for certain limited purposes, can there nevertheless be imposed on auditors an additional common law duty to individual shareholders who choose to use them for another purpose without the prior knowledge of the auditors? The answer must be no .... Only where the auditor was aware that the individual shareholder was likely to rely on the accounts for a particular purpose such as his present or future investment in or lending to the company would a duty of a care arise. Such a situation does not obtain in the present case.

In his judgment, Lord Oliver elaborated on the principle established in *Hedley Byrne*. He stated that the making of a statement will give rise to a duty where (i) advice is sought in circumstances where the advisor is aware, "actually or inferentially," of the purpose for which the advice is sought; (ii) the advisor is aware that the information will be communicated to the other party; (iii) the advisor is aware that the recipient will act on that advice; and (iv) the recipient so acts to his detriment.

4.3 Psychiatric injury

Nervous shock was the phrase commonly used by the legal community to describe cases of psychiatric damage. The use of this phrase betrayed the sceptical attitude of the courts towards this type of injury. In modern times, however, the courts have recognised that the use of such terminology belittles the seriousness of such injury and have recognised that the term "psychiatric damage" is a more appropriate description (*per* Sir Thomas Bingham M.R. in *Attia v. British Gas plc* (1987)).

4.3.1 Liability for psychiatric damage

As in cases involving recovery for pure economic loss, the courts have been reluctant to recognise liability for psychiatric damage based on a straightforward application of the duty of care principle. It was the view that actions for physical injury could be reasonably contained by the concepts of foreseeability, proximity and policy. Psychiatric injury could not, in the courts' view, be easily contained within such restrictions and was treated differently because of the following fears: (i) *faked and exaggerated claims*, namely that the courts were fearful that such injuries could be easily faked, whereas physical injury was easier to prove; (ii) *measurability of damage*, namely that the seriousness of such damage was difficult to quantify; and (iii) *the floodgates argument*, that to allow such claims would lead to a flood of similar actions.

4.3.2 Development of the tort

Initially the courts were reluctant to award damages for psychiatric injury. Medical science had not yet reached the stage where the courts believed that such injury deserved compensation, and in *Victoria Railway Commissioners v. Coultas* (1888), the Privy Council rejected a claim as leaving "a wide field being opened for imaginary claims." An action for negligently caused psychiatric damage was first recognised in Ireland in the case of *Byrne v. Southern and Western Railway Co.* (1884). In that case, the plaintiff narrowly avoided being struck by a train and although "a hair of [his] head was not touched," he received a "fright and shock" and as a result was awarded the sum of £325 in damages. Similarly, in *Bell v. Great Northern Railway Co.* (1890), an action for negligently inflicted psychiatric damage was successful. In finding for the plaintiff, the court acknowledged the seriousness of psychiatric damage, stating that:

> The only questions to be considered, in my opinion, are: was the health or the capacity of the plaintiff for the discharge of her duties and enjoyment of life affected by what occurred to her whilst in the carriage? Next, was this caused by the negligence of the defendants?

Further expansion of the tort occurred with the English decision of *Hambrook v. Stokes Bros.* (1925) where a mother suffered psychiatric trauma when she witnessed a lorry roll down a hill towards her unattended children. Her action was successful. The court found, notwithstanding the fact that the plaintiff was not within the zone of foreseeable physical danger, that she was owed a duty of care. It was the view of the court that if it were reasonably foreseeable that fear for one's own safety could induce psychiatric injury, it was equally foreseeable that fear for the lives of one's children would produce a similar result.

Following the decisions in *Byrne* and *Bell*, the law had moved from a position where it rejected the validity of an action for negligently caused psychiatric damage in *Coultas* to one where a duty for such damage would be held to exist, but only in situations where it was foreseeable that the plaintiff could have suffered physical injury as a result of the defendant's negligence. The judgment in *Hambrook* had extended the duty of care owed to parents who had witnessed the incident although they were not directly involved themselves.

The issue of liability for negligently inflicted psychiatric injury came to prominence once again with the House of Lords decision in *McLoughlin v. O'Brian* (1983). In that case, the plaintiff's husband and their three children had been involved in a traffic accident negligently caused by the defendant. The plaintiff was not present at the scene of the accident and was informed of what had occurred while at home. She rushed to the hospital where she witnessed the surviving members of her family in great distress. The plaintiff suffered severe shock as result of witnessing the aftermath of the accident. Her action for damages for negligently inflicted psychiatric damage against the defendant was successful. However, their Lordships differed in their approaches as to why she should succeed. Whilst Lord Bridge found for the plaintiff based on the basic test of foreseeability, Lord Wilberforce was anxious "to place some limitation on the extent of admissible claims" and suggested that in addition to the requirement of foreseeability that certain policy limitations must be satisfied before a positive finding of duty could be made.

The following limitations, which would only apply where the plaintiff was a secondary victim by virtue of the fact that he did not come within the zone of danger, were identified by Lord Wilberforce. First, the plaintiff must establish that the relationship between the plaintiff and the victim was a close one of love and affection. In relation to parents and their children, husbands and wives, this tie would be presumed. Second, the plaintiff must prove that he was close to the accident in terms of time and space. This requirement would be satisfied where the plaintiff witnessed the incident itself or arrived upon the immediate aftermath of the incident (as the plaintiff in the instant case had done). Finally, the plaintiff must prove that he perceived the accident or its immediate aftermath with his own unaided senses. A third party informing the plaintiff of the incident would be insufficient to create a duty.

Following *McLoughlin*, it was unclear which of the competing approaches adopted by their Lordships in finding for the plaintiff would prevail. The House of Lords' decision in *Alcock v. Chief Constable of South Yorkshire Police* (1992) arose out of the Hillsborough football stadium disaster in 1989, where over 90 football fans died as a result of crushing inside the stadium caused by the defendants' negligence. The plaintiffs were close friends or relatives of the victims and were seeking compensation for negligently inflicted psychiatric damage. Their Lordships, in dismissing each claim, adopted the approach favoured by Lord Wilberforce and agreed that such actions should be limited not by ordinary negligence principles alone. In relation to the requirement to prove the existence of a "close tie of love and affection" as espoused in *McLoughlin*, in *Alcock* the Law Lords agreed that the relationship between spouses and between parents and their children would be presumed to comply with this prerequisite. Lord Keith noted that for other relationships, for example between brothers or brothers-in-law, the plaintiff may be in a position to prove the requisite degree of closeness as a matter of fact. However, Lord Keith noted that, on the facts before him:

> In neither of these cases was there any evidence of particularly close ties of love and affection with the brothers or brothers-in-law. In my opinion, the mere fact of the particular relationship was insufficient to place the plaintiff within the class of persons to whom a duty of

care could be owed by the defendant as being foreseeably at risk of psychiatric illness by reason of injury or peril to the individuals concerned.

The claims of the plaintiffs, who arrived at the scene in the aftermath of the disaster some hours later to identify the bodies of family members in the makeshift morgue, were found not to have been sufficiently close to the accident in time and space to come within the scope of those owed a duty of care. Finally, those plaintiffs who had witnessed the disaster on "live" television were also not owed a duty as they had not directly perceived the incident.

In the House of Lords decision *White v. Chief Constable of South Yorkshire Police* (1999) the plaintiff policemen, who were involved in the Hillsborough Stadium disaster, allegedly suffered nervous shock in the course of carrying out their duties. Their claims in negligence against their employer failed. The courts had tended to treat rescuers such as the plaintiffs as "primary victims" up to that point (*Chadwick v. British Transport Commission* (1967)) thereby exempting them from the rigours of the aftermath test. This tendency was abandoned in *White,* where the Law Lords were emphatic that the aftermath test could not be abrogated by reason of the claimant's categorisation as a rescuer. Therefore, under English law, rescuers who attempt to recover for negligently inflicted psychiatric injury must establish the existence of a close relationship with the primary victim and comply with the other policy requirements introduced by the House of Lords in *McLoughlin v. O'Brian*.

4.4 The Irish position

The cautious attitude which characterised the English courts' approach towards this area reflected the general trend of pragmatism adopted in English negligence law since *Caparo*, whereby a duty would only be recognised in "new" situations in an incremental manner by analogy with other cases. The Irish courts, on the other hand, dealt with such injury in a more flexible manner. In *Mulally v. Bus Éireann* (1992), the plaintiff received a message at home that her husband and three sons had been involved in a serious bus accident. She rushed to the hospital and witnessed terrible scenes of the aftermath of the accident involving her family. Denham J. accepted that the plaintiff was suffering from Post Traumatic Stress Disorder (PTSD), which she said was "a psychiatric disease." The criteria applicable to PTSD were identified as follows:

(i) Exposure to recognisable stress or trauma outside the range of usual human experience, which would evoke significant symptoms of distress in almost anyone;

(ii) Re-experiencing of the trauma through intrusive memories, nightmares or flashbacks or intensification of symptoms through to situations resembling or symbolising the event;

(iii) Avoidance of stimuli related to trauma or numbing of general responsiveness indicated by avoidance of thoughts or feelings, or of situations associated with the trauma, amnesia for important aspects of the trauma, diminished interest in activities, feelings of estrangement from others, constricted effect, sense of foreshortened future;

(iv) Increased arousal indicated by sleep disturbance, anger outbursts, difficulty concentrating, hyper vigilance, exaggerated startle response, psychiatric reactivity to situations resembling or symbolising the trauma;

(v) Duration of disturbance, at least one month.

In finding for the plaintiff, Denham J. avoided a specific discussion of the policy limitations utilised by the House of Lords in both *McLoughlin* and *Alcock*, favouring foreseeability as a test, and as such was "guided more by [the judgment of] Lord Bridge" in *McLoughlin*. She did comment, however, that she was of the view that there was "no policy in Irish law opposed to a finding of nervous shock," and preferred to focus on "whether the causation nexus exist[ed] between the defendants' negligence and the plaintiff's illness" when determining liability.

The Irish Supreme Court considered the matter further in *Kelly v. Hennessy* (1995), where the plaintiff's husband and children were involved in a serious motor accident. The plaintiff was informed of the accident at home and upon arrival at the hospital she witnessed traumatic scenes. Hamilton C.J. set out six principles to determine whether a plaintiff, suffering psychiatric harm, comes within the defendant's duty of care:

(i) The plaintiff must suffer a recognised psychiatric illness;

(ii) The illness must arise by way of shock;

(iii) It must be foreseeable that the initial event could cause psychiatric injury; foreseeability of general personal injury is not enough;

(iv) The illness must result from the perception of actual injury, or a risk of injury to oneself or another person;

(v) If harm results from perception of the aftermath, there must be a close personal relationship between primary victim and plaintiff;

(vi) There are no public policy limits on recovery where the plaintiff established sufficient proximity and foreseeability by fulfilling the above conditions.

The Irish Supreme Court appeared to have adopted the concept of "proximity" as a central element in an action for negligently caused psychiatric damage. The decision in *Kelly* represented a step back from the broader test of mere foreseeability adopted in *Mulally*. The injury must be foreseeable, it must result from perception of the traumatising event, and where the injury results from perception of the aftermath, a close relationship must be established between the plaintiff and the victim. However, it is notable that the Supreme Court did not fully endorse the strict application of the policy limitations favoured in *Alcock*. Indeed, Hamilton C.J. expressly rejected the notion that public policy should necessarily intervene to restrict the action taken by a party who has suffered negligently inflicted psychiatric injury.

5. NEGLIGENCE: THE STANDARD OF CARE

5.1 Introduction

Once it has been established that the plaintiff was owed a duty of care, it must then be proven on a balance of probabilities that the duty has been breached. The defendant will have been found to be in breach of this duty where he has failed to take appropriate care in the given circumstances.

5.2 The reasonable man

The courts have adopted an objective test to determine whether the defendant has taken appropriate care. In order to determine the proper standard of care in any given situation, the courts have enlisted the aid of the hypothetical "reasonable man" (or perhaps more appropriately, "reasonable human being," *per* Kenny J. in *Connolly v. South of Ireland Asphalt Co. Ltd* (1977)). Thus, if a defendant fails to do something which a reasonable man would do in the circumstances, or does something that the reasonable man would not do, he will be deemed to have breached the duty of care owed to the plaintiff (*per* Alderson B. in *Blyth v. Birmingham Waterworks Co.* (1856).

The test is objective and does not take account of individual traits or characteristics. Lord MacMillan in *Glasgow Corporation v. Muir* (1943) stated that:

> The standard of foresight of the reasonable man eliminates the personal equation and is independent of the idiosyncrasies of the particular person whose conduct is in question. Some persons are by nature unduly timorous and imagine every path beset by lions. Others, of more robust temperament, fail to see or nonchalantly disregard even the most obvious dangers. The reasonable man is presumed to be free both from over-apprehension and over-confidence.

Accordingly, the defendant will be compared to an individual "of ordinary intelligence and foresight" (*per* Gavan Duffy J. in *Kirby v. Burke* (1944)). His personal best will be insufficient where it fails to meet the standard of the reasonable man. Thus, the standard of care expected of an inexpert driver, for example, will be that of a reasonable driver of experience, care and skill (*Nettleship v. Weston* (1971)).

While the test is essentially one of objectivity, the standard may vary depending on the circumstances of the case. The question is: what would the reasonable man have foreseen *in the circumstances*? Thus, in *Roe v. Minister for Health* (1954) the plaintiff received a spinal anaesthetic in preparation for an operation. The anaesthetic was contained in a glass vial that was stored in a chemical solution (phenol) for sterilisation purposes. The glass vial contained cracks that were not visible to the eye and as a result the anaesthetic became contaminated. The contaminated anaesthetic caused the plaintiff to suffer from permanent paralysis. At the time of the trial, it was discovered that the contamination would have been easily discovered had the phenol been coloured. However, it was established that at the time of the accident in 1947, it was not known that such invisible cracks could exist, although this fact was widely known by the medical community at the date of the trial. It was held that the doctor in question should be judged according to the knowledge which he reasonably ought to have had at that time of the alleged negligence, *i.e.* 1947. Thus, according to the state of medical knowledge at that time, the defendant was not negligent.

It should be noted that the law does make allowances for certain individual characteristics when determining whether the defendant has failed to meet the requisite standard of care. Thus, a defendant's physical and mental disabilities and his age (where he is not of the age of majority) will be taken into consideration. Therefore, a person who is blind will be judged according to the standard of the reasonable man who is blind and not in accordance with the reasonable man in possession of all his faculties.

5.3 What is the appropriate standard?

In judging the correct standard of care to be attained in any given situation, the courts will take cognisance of a number of factors. These factors (and the weight to be attached to them), which will vary given the circumstances of the particular case, include the probability of the accident occurring, the gravity of the potential harm, the social utility of the defendant's conduct, and the cost of preventing the accident.

5.3.1 Probability

The more likely the accident, the higher the standard of care expected of the defendant. Therefore, in cases of high probability, the defendant must either desist from the conduct in question or take greater precautions to reduce or eliminate the risk which flows from it. In *O'Gorman v. Ritz (Clonmel) Ltd* (1947), the plaintiff attended a showing at the defendant's cinema. She stretched her legs under the seat in front of her. Her leg was cut on the hinge mechanism, when the person sitting in front of her rose from their seat. In determining whether the defendant had failed to meet the requisite standard of care, the court took account of the fact that approximately one million people had visited the cinema in the previous seven years yet no similar complaint had been made. The probability of the accident occurring was therefore quite remote and was a factor that influenced the court in finding that the defendant had not breached the standard of care owed to the plaintiff. Similarly, in *Bolton v. Stone* (1951), the defendants were not found liable where a cricket ball had cleared the outer fence of the cricket field and struck the plaintiff. The judgment of the House of Lords was influenced by the improbability of the accident occurring due to factors such as the distance the ball had travelled and the fact that only on the rarest of occasions had cricket balls cleared the perimeter in the past. In *Keenan v. McCreedy* (1953), it was held that a mill owner producing flax was under a greater duty of care to prevent a fire on his premises, as flax is highly combustible. Therefore, allowing employees to smoke on the premises constituted a breach of the standard of care owed in all the circumstances of the case. Finally, in *Healy v. Bray U.D.C.* (1962), the plaintiff was injured when a rock which became loose, rolled down a hill, through a gap in a wall and struck her. The defendant council was not found liable as "the combination of all these unlikely events [seemed] to reduce the risk to such minute proportions that the Council cannot be held negligent . . ." (*per* Kingsmill Moore J).

5.3.2 Gravity

When examining the defendant's conduct, the courts will have regard to the seriousness or gravity of the harm which may result from the defendant's negligence. In the words of Lord Macmillan in *Read v. Lyons* (1947):

> The law in all cases exacts a degree of care commensurate with the degree of risk created, that is, the greater the risk of harm the more stringent the precautions which must be taken. The magnitude of risk is said to be a product of two factors, the first being the likelihood of the risk materialising, the second being the potential severity of the damage should it occur.

In *Paris v. Stepney Borough Council* (1951), the plaintiff worker only had one eye. In the course of his work, a splinter of metal entered his good eye causing him to lose his sight. The accident occurred as a result of the defendant's failure to provide him with safety goggles. The defendant was found to have breached its duty to the plaintiff. Its duty to take reasonable care in the circumstances was stringent considering the potential gravity of the harm to the plaintiff. The seriousness of the harm was also a determining factor in a finding of breach of duty in *Fitzsimons v. Bord Telecom Éireann and the E.S.B.* (1991), where the plaintiff's husband was killed when he tried to lift a fallen telephone cable from an overhead power line. It was held that as serious injury was a foreseeable consequence of the negligence of the defendants, a higher standard of care was expected, which was not attained in this particular case.

5.3.3 Social utility

The motivation behind the defendant's conduct may be a deciding factor in determining whether the defendant be deemed negligent. As Fleming (1998, p.130) has commented: "there is a world of difference between throwing a burning object into the street below just for the fun of it or in order to save a house on fire." Thus, greater leniency will be displayed in favour of the "good Samaritan" who acts with the best intentions even though he may inadvertently injure another. The social utility of the defendant's conduct must, however, be weighed against the seriousness of the injury. The courts must adopt a balanced approach, for otherwise the operation of everyday life would become impossible. Asquith J. in *Daborn v. Bath Tramways* (1946) explained the dilemma in the following terms:

> If all the trains in this country were restricted to a speed of five miles per hour, there would be fewer accidents, but our national life would be intolerably slowed down. The purpose to be served, if sufficiently important, justifies the assumption of abnormal risk.

In *Watt v. Hertfordshire County Council* (1954), a woman was trapped under a vehicle. The defendant's fire station received an emergency call to the scene of the accident. In order to carry out the rescue of the trapped woman, heavy lifting equipment was required, and the vehicle specifically designed to carry such equipment was out on other service. It was decided in the circumstances to fit the equipment to another vehicle. En route to the scene of the accident, the plaintiff fireman was injured when the equipment (which weighed between two and three hundredweight) moved suddenly. The court found that the defendant was not liable in these circumstances since the plaintiff, by virtue of his occupation, had agreed to assume certain risks, and as "the purpose to be served in this case was the saving of life" the defendant has not breached the duty owed to the plaintiff. Similarly, in *Whooley v. Dublin Corporation* (1961), the plaintiff was injured when, while walking on a footpath, she stepped into an open fire hydrant box. It transpired that the door to the box containing the hydrant had been damaged as the result of vandalism. In finding that the defendants had not breached the standard of care owed to the plaintiff, McLoughlin J. placed particular emphasis on the fact that "no other type of hydrant which could be devised, consistent with the necessary purpose, would be safe from malicious interference."

5.3.4 Cost of prevention

In determining whether the standard has been breached, the law will have regard to the cost that must be incurred in order to eliminate the risk. O'Dalaigh C.J. admitted to such practical considerations in *Kirwan v. Bray U.D.C.* (1969), where he said, "a slight risk may be run if the cost of remedying it is unreasonably high." In *O'Gorman*, the cost of eliminating the risk, by renovating the seating in the cinema, coupled with the low probability of the risk influenced the judgment of the court in finding that the defendant had not breached their duty of care. In *Latimer v. AEC Ltd* (1953), a factory floor was flooded. The floor became very slippery as the water mixed with another oily liquid. A number of the defendant's employees were instructed to cover the floor with sawdust but left a portion uncovered. The plaintiff slipped on the uncovered part. In an action for negligence, the plaintiff argued that the reasonable prudent man would have completely shut down the factory until the spillage had been completely cleaned up. However, the court did not agree that the defendant was required under the common law to take the drastic step of closing down the factory in these circumstances.

The practical implications of placing too onerous a duty on defendants in these circumstances may influence the judgment of the court. In *Muldoon v. Ireland and Others* (1988), the defendant was not found liable for the injuries inflicted on one prisoner by another. In the circumstances, Hamilton J. reasoned that it would be impractical, if not impossible, to search every prisoner for weapons every time they moved from one part of the prison to another. Similarly, in *Sutherland*

6. NEGLIGENCE: CAUSATION AND DAMAGE

6.1 Introduction

In *Weld-Blundell v. Stephens* (1920), Lord Sumner noted that:

> Damage is essential to liability in negligence, and the law has been shaped by many considerations. In the first place, it has to be shown that the damage complained of was caused by the defendant's carelessness. Courts have stressed repeatedly that legal causation is not based on science or philosophy, but on common sense.

In attempting to establish the defendant's liability, the plaintiff must prove that the defendant was both the factual and legal cause of the plaintiff's injury.

6.2 Factual causation

The test which is traditionally favoured when determining the issue of factual causation is the "but for" test. The court asks "would the harm to the plaintiff not have occurred but for the defendant's negligent act or omission?" For example, in *Barnett v. Chelsea & Kensington Hospital Management Committee* (1969), the plaintiff's spouse attended the defendant's out-patient department one New Year's morning complaining of severe pain and vomiting. He was not properly examined by the casualty officer on duty, but instead was advised to see his own doctor later that day. Soon after, he died from arsenic poisoning. However, expert evidence was admitted in evidence that Mr Barnett would have died from the poisoning even if he had received proper care at the defendant's hospital. The "but for" test was not satisfied, the defendant was not the factual cause of the damage suffered by the plaintiff's spouse.

The "but for" test can cause substantial problems where multiple causes operate to bring about the same event or damage. McMahon & Binchy provide the example of two independent fires converging simultaneously on the plaintiff's property. In such a case, the strict application of the "but for" test would mean that neither of the persons responsible for the fires would be liable. The task of attributing liability for causing loss in such scenarios was greatly aided by the development of the "material contribution" test, developed in cases such as

Bonnington Castings v. Wardlaw (1956), and *McGhee v. National Coal Board* (1973). Under this refinement of more orthodox causation principles, causation is established where the breach of duty materially contributed to, rather than solely caused, the plaintiff's injury.

In the more recent Court of Appeal decision in *Page v. Smith* (1995), the plaintiff was suffering from M.E., chronic fatigue syndrome, when the defendant's car negligently crashed into him. The accident had the effect of making the condition chronic and permanent. In refusing the defendant's appeal, the Court of Appeal approved the trial judge's application of the material contribution test in cases such as the present "in which other causes could have played a part in the causation of the plaintiff's exacerbated symptoms."

6.2.1 Novus actus interveniens

The link between the defendant's negligence and the plaintiff's injuries is known as the chain of causation. If this chain is broken by the *novus actus interveniens* (a new intervening act) of a third party, then the damage may be declared to be too remote and as a result the defendant will not be held liable.

In *McKew v. Holland* (1969), the plaintiff was injured as a result of the negligence of the defendants. His injury was slight but it caused him to lose the control of his leg occasionally. Despite this weakness in his left leg, the plaintiff descended a steep flight of stairs which had no handrail. As a result he lost control of his leg, fell down the stairs and broke his ankle. The House of Lords held that the plaintiff's conduct in going down the steep flight unaided was unreasonable and had the effect of breaking the chain of causation. Lord Reid stated, "if the injured man acts unreasonably, he cannot hold the defendant liable for injury caused by his own unreasonable conduct."

The *McKew* case can be compared with *Wieland v. Cyril Lord Carpets* (1969), where the plaintiff suffered an injury to her neck as a result of the defendant's negligence. As a consequence of her injury, a surgical collar was fitted which restricted her ability to move her head and she was unable to use her bifocal lenses as before. While in this condition she fell down a flight of stairs. Eveleigh J. held that the defendant was liable for the injury which the plaintiff sustained on falling down the stairs. He stated that this was a case where the plaintiff had, as a result of the accident, been left unable to cope with the "vicissitudes of life," and the defendant was liable for the further injury which she suffered while in this condition.

A rather harsh application of the *novus actus interveniens* principle occurred in the case of *Felloni v. Dublin Corporation* (1998). Here the plaintiff, a 15-year-old girl, injured her finger when closing a door. The door had been fitted with a knocker, the use of which would have avoided the accident, but at the time of the accident this knocker was defective. Morris J. considered the failure of the occupier (the plaintiff's aunt) to inform the defendant landlord of the defect to be a *novus actus interveniens*. This decision is criticised by Byrne & Binchy (*Annual Review of Irish Law,* 1997, p. 756) on the basis that:

> the relationship between landlord and tenant is ongoing; it does not consist of an initial provision of premises to the tenant, for which the defendant must thereafter take over responsibility … A reduction for contributory negligence would seem a sufficient sanction.

In *Lamb v. Camden Borough Council* (1981), the defendant, by its negligence, damaged a water main outside the plaintiff's house. This resulted in major subsidence of the house. As a consequence, the plaintiff tenant moved out and shortly afterwards squatters moved in and inflicted substantial damage on the property. The plaintiff sought to recover from the defendant for this damage. The Court of Appeal held that the plaintiff could not recover, but had difficulty justifying the decision. Lord Denning decided the issue on policy grounds, whereas the other members of the Court held that the damage was too remote a consequence of the defendant's negligence. Olivier L.J. stated (at p. 419): "it was inconceivable that the reasonable man, wielding his pick in the road in 1973, could be said reasonably to foresee that his puncturing of a water main would fill the plaintiff's house with uninvited guests in 1974."

6.3 Legal causation – remoteness of damage

A plaintiff, faced with the task of establishing the defendant's liability, and having proven that the defendant was responsible for the factual cause for his loss, must take the vital further step of establishing legal causation. What if the resultant damage turns out to be more extensive or of a different type or occurred in a different way from that which might reasonably be expected to arise from the defendant's conduct? Remoteness of damage is the criteria which the courts use in fixing the cut-off point in the line of consequences, beyond which the defendant will not be legally accountable.

There was always some authority for the proposition that a wrong-doer is liable only for damage which was intended by him or which, though not intended, was the natural and probable consequence of his unlawful act. This test of reasonable foreseeability having been decisively rejected by the Court of Appeal in *Re Polemis* (1921), was just as decisively accepted and restored to favour by the Judicial Committee of the Privy Council in *The Wagon Mound* (1961).

In *Re Polemis,* the direct consequence test had been adopted. It was held that if the damage caused was a direct consequence of the defendant's negligent act, then the defendant will be held liable for same. It was irrelevant that the defendant could not have anticipated the extent of the damage. This approach differentiates between the test to determine whether liability exists (foreseeability) and the test for limiting the extent of liability (directness of consequence). In *Re Polemis,* two workmen negligently dropped a plank into the hold of a ship. The impact caused a spark, which ignited petrol vapours and caused an explosion which destroyed the ship. The owners sued the ship's charterers (who employed the two workmen) and it was held that the charterers were liable for all the direct or natural consequences of their negligent act.

Some light was later thrown upon the meaning of direct cause by the House of Lords' decision in *Liesbosch Dredger (Owners) v. Edison (Owners)* (1932). A dredger was sunk owing to the negligence of the Edison. The owners of the dredger required it for the performance of a contract, delay in the completion of which exposed them to heavy penalties. Owing to a want of funds, they could not purchase a dredger to take the place of the Liesbosch, and were forced to hire one at an exorbitant rate. It was held that the increased loss which the plaintiffs suffered due to their impecuniosity could not be recovered. However decisions such as *Perry v. Sidney Phillips* (1982) and *Archer v. Brown* (1985) illustrate the fact that the *Liesbosch* decision was never fully accepted by the courts. In *Doran v. Delaney (No. 2)* (1999), Geoghegan J. refused to limit the damages payable to the plaintiffs on the basis that "extra" harm was caused to them due to their impecuniosity. He said:

> ... it seems clear from *McGregor on Damages* that the English courts have been gradually whittling away any idea that impecuniosity cannot be taken into account .... Loss is not too remote if it could have been reasonably within the contemplation of the parties at the time of entering into the contract ...

In *The Wagon Mound (No. 1)* (*Overseas Tankship (U.K.) Ltd v. Morts Dock and Engineering* (1961)), the Privy Council described the

Polemis approach as "fundamentally false". Here the steamship Wagon Mound was taking in bunkering oil some 600 feet away from a wharf in Sydney Harbour. As a result of the carelessness of those on board, a large quantity of oil spilt into the bay. Some 60 hours later, that oil ignited and a fire spread rapidly and did considerable damage to the wharf and also to ships adjoining the wharf. The outbreak of fire was due to the fact that wind and tide had together carried under the wharf some inflammable debris, on top of which lay some cotton waste, which was then set alight by molten metal falling from the wharf as a result of welding operations being carried out on it. These flames in turn set the floating oil alight. The Judicial Committee held that the test of remoteness of damage was reasonable foreseeability and, on the facts, the damage in question was not reasonably foreseeable at all. The Privy Council stated that it was illogical and unjust to adopt two different standards, one for determining liability, the other for setting a limit on the damage recoverable. Instead there should be one uniform test of liability and remoteness, the reasonable foreseeability test.

The *Wagon Mound* decision met with an immediately favourable response from the Irish judiciary, as evidenced by decisions such as *Riordans Travel v. Acres & Co.* (1979), *Burke v. John Paul & Co.*(1967) and *Condon v. C.I.E.*(1984, High Court). McMahon & Binchy (2000 at p. 88) note that the Irish courts disenchantment with *Re Polemis* was evident as early as 1960, in the form of the Supreme Court decision in *O'Mahoney v. Ford* (1962).

Much of the case law on remoteness of damage has been concerned with rescuers who have suffered injury where the rescue was necessitated by the defendant's negligence. Traditionally, the courts took a defendant-friendly approach by considering a rescuer's conscious exposure of himself to injury to be a *novus actus interveniens*. For example, in *Horsley v. MacLaren,* a 1972 Supreme Court of Canada decision, it was held that a passenger who jumped from a boat to rescue a friend who had fallen overboard could not recover under the tort of negligence because his decision to jump into the icy waters of Lake Ontario was not reasonably foreseeable. However, liability was imposed in *Turner v. Irish Rail* (1996), where a mother fell on the railway track when searching agitatedly for her six year old daughter whom she mistakenly believed to have gone through an opening in the fence beside the track. Flood J. imposed liability on the railway company and local authority for negligently creating the situation of apparent danger.

McMahon & Binchy (2000, p.97) note that:

> although not totally free from doubt, the better opinion suggests that
> the direct consequences of *Re Polemis* may still survive in the strict
> torts. In *Wagon Mound (No 1)* itself it is suggested that the reasonable
> foreseeability test might not apply to *Rylands v. Fletcher*. And the
> Supreme Court in Ireland and the Court of Appeal in England have
> ruled that the direct consequences rule of *Polemis* applies to deceit.

6.4 The egg-shell skull rule

There is a general rule in tort law to the effect that the defendant must
take his victim as he finds him. Therefore, if the plaintiff suffers much
greater damage, due to some physical or psychological predisposition
on his part, then the defendant will be liable for the full range of actual
damage that results. The "egg-shell skull" rule is an exception to the
general rule that damage must be reasonably foreseeable in order to be
recoverable. The rule survived the introduction of the reasonable foreseeability test in *Wagon Mound (No. 1)* and provides that, as far as the
physical, financial or emotional condition of the victim is concerned,
abnormal circumstances existing at the time of the wrongful act do not
negative causal connection. So for example in *Smith v. Leech Brain &
Co. Ltd* (1962), it was held that if a victim of a negligent act suffers
from a pre-cancerous condition which is activated by that negligent act,
the wrongdoer is responsible for all the disastrous consequences.

In *Burke v. John Paul & Co.* (1967), the plaintiff was an employee of
the defendant who was injured while cutting steel bars with a hand-
operated cutter. The blades were blunt and forced the plaintiff to exert a
greater physical effort than should have been necessary. The plaintiff
had complained about the inadequate sharpness, but without response
from his employer. On the day of the accident, the plaintiff felt a snap
internally, caused by the occurrence of a hernia-related condition. The
defendant sought a direction at the end of the plaintiff's case that they
could not reasonably anticipate that the plaintiff would suffer a hernia
because of his exertions. They might have anticipated muscle tear or
strain, but not the hernia which was due to a congenital predisposition
of the plaintiff. The Supreme Court rejected this argument and held the
defendant liable.

In *McCarthy v. Murphy* (1998), McCracken J. was called on to consider the application of the rule in circumstances where physical and
mental injury intersected. The plaintiff, when seated in a stationary car,
was struck from behind by the defendant's vehicle. Although the

impact was very slight, she suffered a mild to moderate soft-tissue injury. She later developed a serious depressive reaction, which was partly attributable to a pre-existing underlying depressive condition. The defendant argued that he was liable only for injury of a type that was reasonably foreseeable, and that it was not foreseeable that any form of psychological injury would occur as a result of a very minor traffic accident such as had occurred. McCracken J. rejected this argument, regarding it as "totally at odds" with the Supreme Court decision in *Burke*.

Finally, it should be noted that if the defendant intended to cause the damage which resulted, he is automatically liable, regardless of the fact that he may not have regarded it as a reasonably foreseeable consequence of his actions. So, in *Quinn v. Leatham* (1901), Lord Lindley stated that intention "disposes of any question of remoteness of damage."

6.5 The doctrine of *res ipsa loquitur*

Literally translated as "the thing speaks for itself," the doctrine is reputed to trace its origin to an off-hand remark to counsel by Pollock C.B. during the course of argument in *Byrne v. Boadle* (1863).

The rule that it is for the plaintiff to prove negligence, and not for the defendant to disprove it, is in some cases one of considerable hardship to the plaintiff, because it may be that the true cause of the accident lies solely within the knowledge of the defendant who caused it. This hardship is avoided to a considerable extent by the principle of *res ipsa loquitur* where a court will, in exceptional circumstances, draw an inference of negligence on the basis of circumstantial evidence of a highly suggestive nature. The *locus classicus* in this area is *Scott v. London and St. Katherine Docks Co.* (1861), where the plaintiff was passing under a loading bay of the defendant's warehouse when sacks of sugar fell from the bay and landed on him. In holding that in these circumstances, negligence on the part of the defendant would be presumed, the court stipulated as conditions for the operation of the principle that (i) the thing be shown to be under the management of the defendant or his servants, and (ii) that the accident is such as in the ordinary course of things does not happen if those who have the management use proper care.

In *Foley v. Quinnsworth* (1992), it was held that the doctrine did not apply in circumstances where the plaintiff slipped on a floor on which no spillages could be found immediately afterwards.

The decision of the Supreme Court in *Lindsay v. Mid Western Health Board* (1993) involved a plaintiff who was eight years old when admitted to a hospital owned and operated by the defendant. An emergency appendectomy was carried out while she was under a general anaesthetic, from which she never regained consciousness. At the time of the hearing in the High Court, she had been in a deep coma for over 18 years. On appeal, the Supreme Court, in denying the applicability of the doctrine to the facts of the case, emphasised the need for evidence of an extraordinary event which would not normally occur if due care was being taken. The court stated that the rule embodied in the maxim *res ipsa loquitur* must not place so onerous a burden on a defendant that unjust results would be produced. It would be an unjustifiable extension of the law to say that negligence on the part of a defendant must be inferred in the absence of an explanation for the injury which could be proved by the defendant on the balance of probabilities. The defendant was therefore not required to take the further step of proving on the balance of probabilities what had caused the plaintiff's injuries.

In *Neill v. Minister for Finance* (1948), the plaintiff (who at the time of the accident was just over two years of age) injured his hand when a postman shut the post van door on it. Black J. rejected the plea of *res ipsa loquitur* stating, "I cannot see how the *res ipsa loquitur* principle can be applied in the present case. The gap which exists between the evidence as to the movements of the driver and the injury of the child could be filled in a number of ways." Another case, where a claim to *res ipsa loquitur* was rejected by the courts, is *McDonagh v. West of Ireland Fisheries* (1986). The plaintiff's fishing boat was removed from its berth and later re-berthed by the defendant's employees. At this point it was found to be damaged. The plaintiff's assertion that the doctrine of *res ipsa loquitur* was applicable was rejected by the High Court. In the circumstances, the "thing," the damage caused to the boat, did not speak for itself.

The High Court and the Supreme Court denied the relevance of the doctrine to the facts of *Hanrahan v. Merck, Sharpe & Dohme Ltd* (1988). In the words of Henchy J:

> ... [t]he ordinary rule is that a person who alleges a particular tort must, in order to succeed, prove (save where there are admissions) all the necessary ingredients of that tort and it is not for the defendant to disprove anything. Such exceptions as have been allowed to that general rule seem to be confined to cases where a particular element of the tort lies, or is deemed to lie, pre-eminently within the defendant's knowledge, in which case the onus of proof as to that matter passes to

the defendant. Thus, in the tort of negligence, where damage has been caused to the plaintiff in circumstances in which such damage would not usually be caused without negligence on the part of the defendant, the rule of *res ipsa loquitur* will allow the act relied on to be evidence of negligence in the absence of proof by the defendant that it occurred without want of due care on his part. The rationale behind the shifting of the onus of proof to the defendant in such cases would appear to lie in the fact that it would be palpably unfair to require a plaintiff to prove something which is beyond his reach and which is peculiarly within the range of the defendant's capacity of proof.

In *Duffy v. North Eastern Health Board* (1988), a surgeon employed by the defendant carried out an operation on the plaintiff's leg. A number of days afterwards, the plaintiff lost some sensation in his left hand. It was argued on his behalf that the *res ipsa loquitur* doctrine was applicable, this contention was rejected by the High Court which held that the plaintiff had failed to show that in the ordinary course of events the injury would not have occurred if due care had been taken by the surgeon.

7. NEGLIGENCE: DEFENCES

7.1 Introduction

The defences of contribution, voluntary assumption of risk, and illegality are considered in this chapter due to their particular relevance in the tort of negligence, although they are also frequently relied on by parties to actions based in other torts, such as trespass, defamation and nuisance.

7.2 Contributory negligence

The contributory negligence defence signifies the way in which the plaintiff's own want of care has contributed to the damage which he has suffered. McMahon & Binchy (2000 at p. 560) describe this partial defence as:

> A plaintiff's failure to exercise reasonable care for his own protection will not amount to contributory negligence in respect of damage unless that damage results from the particular risk to which his conduct exposed him. In other words, the fact that the plaintiff has been careless for his own safety in one respect will not assist the defendant unless that carelessness gave rise to a risk of injury that in fact transpired.

Prior to the enactment of the Civil Liability Act 1961, contributory negligence was an absolute defence. Under section 34(1) of that Act:

> … [w]here, in any action brought by one person in respect of a wrong committed by any other person, it is proved that the damage suffered by the plaintiff was caused partly by the negligence or want of care of the plaintiff or of one for whose acts he is responsible (in this part called Contributory Negligence) and partly by the wrong of the defendant, the damages recoverable in respect of the said wrong shall be reduced by such amount as the court thinks just and equitable having regard to the degrees of fault of the plaintiff and defendant.

In this context, "fault" is equated with moral blameworthiness "measured against the degree of capacity or knowledge which such person ought to have had if he were an ordinary, reasonable person" (*per* Walsh J. in *O'Sullivan v. Dwyer* (1971)).

Under section 34(2)(b) of the Civil Liability Act 1961, a negligent or careless failure to mitigate damage is deemed to be contributory negligence in respect of the amount by which such damage exceeds the damage that would otherwise have occurred.

In *Heatley v. Wicklow Urban District Council and Electricity Supply Board* (1998), O'Donovan J. acquitted the plaintiff pedestrian of contributory negligence in failing to see the stump of an old electricity pole which had not been fully removed when a replacement pole was installed. The stump was on a footpath, hidden from the plaintiff's view by the new pole until he was actually on top of it. O'Donovan J. considered that:

> [i]n any event the [stump] which was responsible for the Plaintiff's fall would only have been seen by him if he had been looking to the ground as he walked along and I do not think that the was under any obligation to keep looking at the ground all the time.

In *Hegarty v. Donegal County Council*, (1998), O'Sullivan J. denied that the plaintiff pedestrian had contributed to his loss in failing to see a small step on the pavement which was "not visible on reasonable care being taken" by her.

It should be noted that where it is not possible to establish different degrees of fault between the parties, liability will be apportioned equally. Under section 42 of the 1961 Act, the court is encouraged to have cognisance of the apportioned liability in determining the costs to be awarded against the defendant. The contribution of one party may be attributed to the plaintiff in a number of situations, for example, where the plaintiff is vicariously liable for that party's actions, or where the plaintiff is not the immediate victim of the wrong, *e.g.* the victim's personal representatives.

7.3 The voluntary assumption of risk

The latin phrase *volenti non fit injuria* denotes a voluntary assumption of risk on the part of the plaintiff, which then relieves the defendant of liability for the damage which has accrued to the plaintiff. The defence is rarely successful and is now governed by the terms of section 34(1)(b) of the Civil Liability Act 1961.

Section 34 (1)(b) provides that section 34(1), which deals with contributory negligence:

> … shall not operate to defeat any defence arising under a contract or the defence that the plaintiff before the act complained of agreed to

waive his legal rights in respect of it, whether or not for value, but, subject as aforesaid, the provisions of this subsection shall apply notwithstanding that the defendant might, apart from this subsection, have the defence of voluntary assumption of risk.

The *volenti* defence was frequently relied on by employers as a means of preventing their employees from recovering damages in negligence in connection with injuries sustained in the workplace. So for instance, miners were deemed to have voluntarily assumed the risks inherent in working in a mine, and the phrase "inherent risk" was broadly interpreted. Section 34(1)(b) of the Civil Liability Act 1961 has altered the law in this area by limiting the range of circumstances in which a defendant can plead that the plaintiff consented to the risk which caused the injury. The defendant can escape liability in two cases, (i) contract, and (ii) agreement.

7.3.1 Contract

In *O'Hanlon v. E.S.B.*, Walsh J. noted that:

It is already settled that such contracts are construed strictly against the party claiming the benefit of the exception and there are instances where such contracts are actually prohibited by statute.

7.3.2 Agreement

According to Walsh J., "agreement" in this context:

[n]ecessarily contemplates some sort of intercourse or communication between the plaintiff and the defendants from which it could be reasonably inferred that the plaintiff had assured the defendants that he waived any right of action he might have in respect of the negligence of the defendants. A one-sided secret determination on the part of the plaintiff to give up his right of action for negligence would not amount to an agreement to do so. Such a determination or consent may be regarded as a "voluntary assumption of risk" in the terms of the Act but, by virtue of the provisions of the Act and for the purposes of the Act, this would be contributory negligence and not the absolute defence mentioned in the first part of subs.1(b) of section 34. There are considerable difficulties in determining whether there was any sort of intercourse or communication between the plaintiff and the defendant from which it could reasonably be inferred that the plaintiff had informed the [defendant] that he waived any right of action he might have.

In *O'Hanlon v. E.S.B.* (1969), the concept was characterised as "the defence that the plaintiff, before the act complained of, agreed to waive his legal rights in respect of it." It was stated that the word "agreed" in the section necessarily contemplated some sort of intercourse or communication between the parties from which it could reasonably be inferred that the plaintiff had assured the defendant he had waived any right of action which he might have in respect of the defendant's negligence. The Court went on to say that a one-sided determination on the part of the plaintiff to give up his action would not amount to an agreement to do so.

In *Regan v. Irish Automobile Club* (1990), the plaintiff was employed by the defendants to officiate as a flag marshal at a car race in the Phoenix Park. Prior to the race, she signed a form under which she agreed to act in an official capacity and to absolve all persons having any connection with the promotion or organisation of the meeting (including the R.I.A.C.) from liability arising out of any accident however caused to her person or property. She was then sent to act as flag marshal at the end of the fastest straight (on a hair-pin bend). She was injured when a car went out of control at the bend and hit her. The High Court held that the plaintiff's claim was barred by the defence of *volenti non fit injuria*.

7.4 Illegality

Section 57(1) of the Civil Liability Act 1961 provides that "it shall not be a defence in an action merely to show that the plaintiff is in breach of the civil or criminal code." By virtue of the use of the word "merely," it is clear that the common law defence of *ex turpi causa non oritur actio* (no action arises from a base cause) has not been abolished by section 57(1). Rather, it emphasises that the mere fact the defendant can show the plaintiff is in breach of the law is not, of itself, a defence. In determining the circumstances in which the plaintiff's illegality will be such as to convince a court to refuse his claim, a test of "public conscience" has been developed. Under this test, public policy is predominant. The court is justified in dismissing the plaintiff's claim if, to do otherwise, would have the effect of encouraging his wrongdoing (*Euro-Diam v. Bathurst* (1990)).

8. DEFAMATION

8.1 Introduction

The right of freedom of expression is guaranteed under Article 40.6.1°
of the Constitution, which provides that:

> The State guarantees liberty for the exercise of the following right,
> subject to public order and morality:– (i) The right of the citizens to
> express freely their convictions and opinions ...

This right is not unlimited. In order to ensure that Article 40.6.1° is not
abused to the detriment of another's reputation, Article 40.3.2° provides that:

> The State shall, in particular, by its laws protect as best it may from
> unjust attack and, in the case of injustice done, vindicate the ... good
> name ... of every citizen.

Thus Irish law recognises two rights which could potentially become
diametrically opposed to each other. It is the function of the courts to
ensure that a balance is struck between these competing rights. The tort
of defamation seeks to assist the courts in effecting such a balance. The
tort recognises the need for freedom of expression, but also insists that
the exercise of this right must not unfairly come at the expense of
another's reputation. The importance of an individual's reputation was
highlighted by Lord Nicholls in *Reynolds v. Times Newspapers Ltd*
(1999) when he stated that:

> ...[r]eputation is an integral and important part of the dignity of the
> individual. It also forms the basis of many decisions in a democratic
> society which are fundamental to its well-being: whom to employ or
> work for, whom to promote, whom to do business with or to vote for.
> Once besmirched by an unfounded allegation in a national newspaper,
> a reputation can be damaged for ever, especially if there is no oppor-
> tunity to vindicate one's reputation. When this happens, society as
> well as the individual is the loser. For it should not be supposed that
> protection of reputation is a matter of importance only to the affected
> individual and his family. Protection of reputation is conducive to the
> public good. It is in the public interest that the reputation of public
> figures should not be debased falsely ... freedom of expression is not
> an absolute right. Its exercise may be subject to such restrictions as

are prescribed by law and are necessary in a democratic society for the protection of the reputations of others.

Irish defamation law is primarily derived from the common law, although the Defamation Act 1961 was successful in eliminating many of the subtle distinctions which were the hallmark of this area prior to the limited form of codification effected by the Act. Further statutory reform has been proposed by the Law Reform Commission in its 1991 Report. However, these proposals have yet to be implemented.

The Defamation Act 1961 does not provide a definition of what amounts to a defamatory statement. Thus one must rely on the common law definition provided by the Supreme Court in *Quigley v. Creation Ltd* (1971):

> Defamation is committed by the wrongful publication of a false statement about a person, which tends to lower that person in the eyes of right-thinking members of society or tends to hold that person up to hatred, ridicule or contempt, or causes that person to be shunned or avoided by right-thinking members of society (*per* Walsh J.).

This definition is an elaboration of that provided by Lord Atkin in *Sim v. Stretch* (1936), a House of Lords decision. The *Quigley* definition makes explicit the requirements of publication and falsity. O'Dell ("Does Defamation Value Free Expression?" (1990) 12 D.U.L.J. (ns) 50) has pointed out that the tort is one of strict liability in that if a statement is false, then the publisher is liable regardless of fault.

8.2. Publication

The defamatory statement must be published if the plaintiff is to succeed. Publication in this context means that the statement must be communicated to a third party.

8.2.1 Forms of publication

There are two forms of publication giving rise to separate actions in defamation, namely, libel and slander. Libel is defamation in a permanent form, for example statements published in a newspaper or book, made on film or radio. By virtue of its permanency, such defamation is generally treated as the more serious of the two forms of publication. Slander, on the other hand, is made in a transient form, for example a defamatory statement made orally or by way of a gesture to another.

The distinction between these forms of publication has practical repercussions. Libel is a criminal offence, and is actionable *per se* while slander is only actionable on proof of actual damage. In *Davies v. Solomon* (1871), the loss of the hospitality of a friend was considered to be actionable damage for these purposes.

There are a number of exceptions to the general rule that slander is not actionable *per se*.

8.2.1.1 Slanders imputing unchastity in a woman or a girl

Section 16 of the Defamation Act 1961 provides that words imputing unchastity in a woman or girl shall be actionable *per se*. It is noteworthy that similar protection is not afforded against allegations of unchastity against men under the Act. The constitutionality of this section may be questioned in light of the Irish Constitution's guarantee of equality. From *Kerr v. Kennedy* (1942), it would appear that section 16 would include allegations concerning the commission of lesbian acts.

8.2.1.2 Slanders affecting a person's professional or occupational reputation

Slanders that affect a person's professional or occupational reputation, because of their potential to cause damage, were considered to be actionable *per se*. In *Bennett v. Quane* (1948), a statement alleging that a solicitor brought an action in a higher court in order to obtain a higher level of costs for himself was considered to be slanderous and was actionable *per se* under this exception.

8.2.1.3 Slanders alleging the commission of a crime

Slanders which allege the commission of a crime punishable by a term of imprisonment are considered to be actionable *per se*. It would appear that the serious nature of such slanders, which could cause a person to be ostracised from society, justifies this exception (*Gray v. Jones* (1939)).

In *Monson v. Tussauds Ltd* (1894), it was held that a waxwork model of the plaintiff placed in the Chamber of Horrors amounted to a defamatory publication in circumstances where the plaintiff had recently been the accused in a well-publicised murder trial.

8.2.1.4 Slanders imputing a contagious disease

Any slander which imputed that a person had a contagious disease
(such as AIDS, T.B. etc) are actionable *per se*. Once again, the rationale for this exception would appear to lie in the seriousness of the allegation. In *Bloodworth v. Gray* (1844), a slanderous statement that the
plaintiff had contracted smallpox was actionable by him without showing actionable damage.

8.2.2 Liability

A defendant will be liable in defamation, even where he is not the original publisher of the defamatory statement, where he repeats a defamatory statement made by another. Thus, in *Berry v. Irish Times Ltd*
(1973), the defendant newspaper reproduced a photograph of a man
holding a placard containing a defamatory statement about the plaintiff. The production of the photograph by *The Irish Times* was found to
be publication and the newspaper was found liable for the publication.

It is no defence for the publisher of a defamatory statement to state
that it was made clear in their publication that the statement was a mere
rumour and that its accuracy could not be completely relied upon
(*Stern v. Piper* (1996)).

It would appear that communications between a husband and wife
do not amount to publication for the purposes of the tort (*Wennhak v.
Morgan* (1888)). However, defamatory publications made by a third
party to one spouse concerning the other are actionable at the suit of
the defamed spouse (*Wenman v. Ash* (1853)). The historical rationale
for the former rule was that a husband and wife were treated as one in
the eyes of the law. It would seem that the modern rationale for this rule
lies in the promotion of the institution of marriage.

8.2.3 Accidental publication

A publisher will be held liable under the tort of defamation where the
defamatory statement was published through negligence or want of
care. Thus, in *Paul v. Holt* (1935), a defamatory letter was addressed to
a Mr Paul at an address in "Adavoyle, Meigh, Newry." The plaintiff's
brother who happened to live at the same address opened the letter. He
then showed it to his wife and to the plaintiff's wife. The defendant was
found liable for the publication, notwithstanding the fact that it was
entirely accidental. Evidence was introduced showing that the defendant was aware that the plaintiff's brother lived at the same address.

8.2.4 Innocent dissemination

The general principle is that every publication of a defamatory state-ment creates a fresh cause of action. Furthermore, the original pub-lisher of a defamatory statement may be liable for its republication by another person where the republication of the words to a third party was a natural and probable consequence of the original publication. This is known as the rule in *Speight v. Gospay* (1891).

The law has recognised that the rule in *Speight v. Gospay* has the capacity to create great injustice in certain situations. The so-called "mechanical publisher's" defence, as illustrated in such decisions as *Fitzgibbon v. Eason & Sons Ltd* (1910), does much to alleviate the rigidity of the rule for certain defendants such as booksellers and news-agents. In the *Fitzgibbon* case, it was stated that:

> The vendor of a newspaper who, in the ordinary course of business sells or distributes a paper containing a libel, is *prima facie* liable, but can escape liability by showing that he did not know and had no grounds for thinking that the matter was libellous, and that his igno-rance was not due to negligence.

The onus is on the publisher in such situations to prove his innocence (*Ross v. Eason & Sons Ltd* (1911)).

8.3 Defamatory statement

If the plaintiff is to succeed in an action for defamation, he must estab-lish that the statement has a defamatory effect. In *Quigley v. Creation Ltd* (1971), a magazine purported to publish an interview with an Irish actor, entitled "They left this Isle," although no such interview had ever taken place. The plaintiff argued that the title of the fictitious article implied that he left the country not for the love of his art, but purely for financial gain. The Court agreed, holding that the statement was defamatory.

It is clear from the definition provided by Walsh J. in *Quigley*, that the test for establishing whether a statement is defamatory or not is an objective one. If the false statement would tend to injure the reputation of the person in the eyes of right-thinking members of society, then it will be considered defamatory. An example of the application of this objective test is *Berry v. Irish Times Ltd* (1973), where the defendant published a photograph of a protestor holding a placard which read: "Peter Berry 20th Century Felon Setter – Helped jail Republicans in

England." It was held that the words published by the newspaper were not defamatory as they were not such as would lower the plaintiff (the Secretary to the Department of Justice) in the eyes of right-thinking members of society. In *Byrne v. Deane* (1937), police raided a golf clubhouse and removed illegal gaming machines. Following the raid, the defendant allegedly posted a verse in the clubhouse, which the plaintiff claimed implied that he had acted as police informant in relation to the machines' presence. It was held that the verse did not amount to defamation, for a statement which implies that an individual assisted the police in the prevention of crime could not be deemed to have lowered that individual in the eyes of right-thinking members of society, even if it did affect his popularity and spoil the entertainment of some club members.

The defamatory statement need not imply misconduct or ineptitude in order to be actionable. A statement which tends to hold the plaintiff up to ridicule or contempt will also be regarded as defamatory. In the words of Neill L.J. in *Berkoff v. Burchill* (1996):

> ... words may be defamatory, even though they neither impute disgraceful conduct to the plaintiff nor any lack of skill or efficiency in the conduct of his trade or professional activity, if they hold him up to contempt, scorn or ridicule or tend to exclude him from society.

In that case, the defendant, a journalist, published a review of a play by the plaintiff, actor/director Stephen Berkoff and made certain comments to the effect that the plaintiff, Mr Berkoff, was "hideously ugly." The Court accepted that the comments attributed to the defendant could damage the reputation of the plaintiff since to make such a statement concerning:

> ... someone in the public eye who makes his living, in part at least, as an actor, is capable of lowering his standing in the estimation of the public and of making him an object of ridicule.

It is clear that the impugned statement should be examined in light of the words published, the person concerned, and the general circumstances in which the statement was made. In *Reynolds v. Malocco, t/a "Patrick"* (1999), the plaintiff owned various Dublin nightclubs. He sought an injunction to prevent the publication of an article in the defendant's magazine, which referred to him as a "gay bachelor". Kelly J. rejected the defendant's contention that the word "gay" in its ordinary meaning is an adjective to describe someone who is vivacious, joyful, fond of pleasure and gaiety, stating that:

Language is a living thing and words can change their meaning over the years ... [a] word may acquire a secondary meaning which it did not formerly have ... Over the last thirty years or so [gay] has become synonymous with homosexuals and homosexual activity. One would have to be resident on the moon not to be aware of this.

8.3.1 Vulgar abuse

Generally, mere vulgar abuse will not amount to defamation, since the use of abusive words has become so commonplace in everyday vernacular, particularly when uttered in the heat of the moment, that they should not be understood as commentary on the quality of an individual's character. Thus in *Hoebergen v. Koppens* (1929), it was held that to call someone a "Dutch bastard" was mere vulgar abuse and not to be taken as a comment questioning the plaintiff's parentage.

8.3.2 Innuendo

As noted in *Reynolds v. Malocco* (1999), the words alleged to be defamatory will be given their ordinary and natural meaning. However, words that are not on their face critical of the plaintiff may be deemed to be defamatory if they bear an adverse secondary meaning.

There are two forms of innuendo recognised, the false innuendo and the true innuendo. The former is deemed to have been published where an individual can "read between the lines" of the statement and garner another meaning which may be considered defamatory. In *Campbell v. Irish Press Ltd* (1955), the plaintiff was in the business of providing snooker equipment. He organised an exhibition featuring a famous snooker player. A review of the exhibition was published in the defendant's newspaper, which stated that the snooker player failed to reach a century break because "the table told lies," in other words because the table was unfit for play. The plaintiff alleged that this comment was defamatory because it implied that he had ineptly organised the exhibition. The Court agreed.

A true innuendo is a statement made which, although completely innocent on its face, may be defamatory when read in light of certain extrinsic facts. So, in *Cassidy v. Daily Mirror Newspaper Ltd* (1929), a photograph of a woman and the plaintiff's husband was published by the defendant over the caption "Mr. Cassidy who recently got engaged to Miss X." The plaintiff successfully argued that this publication was defamatory since it implied that she was not married to Mr Cassidy but was instead living immorally with him. Similarly, in *Tolley v. Fry &*

Sons Ltd (1931), a cartoon featured the plaintiff, a well-known amateur golfer. In the cartoon he was depicted as promoting Fry's chocolate. The plaintiff successfully claimed that the cartoon was defamatory since it implied that he was prostituting his amateur status by accepting money to promote the defendant's product.

8.3.3 The statement must refer to the plaintiff

The defamatory statement must refer to the plaintiff, in the sense that he must be readily identifiable from it. The test is whether the ordinary sensible person would be reasonably likely to understand that the statement referred to the plaintiff. The plaintiff need not be expressly named in the defamatory statement. In *Sinclair v. Gogarty* (1937), the defendant in his book *As I was walking down Sackville Street* made a defamatory reference to "two Jews on Sackville Street." It was held that an ordinary sensible person could reasonably identify the plaintiff from this statement. In *Fullam v. Associated Newspapers Ltd* (1955–56), evidence that a crowd jeered a footballer following the publication of the impugned article was held to be good evidence that the plaintiff had been identified as being the subject of the offending article.

It is no defence for the publisher to say that the statement was not intended to refer to the plaintiff and that any perceived connection was mere coincidence. In the words of Lord Loreburn in *E. Hulton & Co. v. Jones* (1910):

> A man in good faith may publish a libel believing it to be true, and it may be found by the jury that he acted in good faith believing it to be true, and reasonably believing it to be true, but that in fact the statement was false. Under those circumstances he has no defence to the action, however excellent his intention.

In that case, the defendant published what was intended to be a fictional article regarding one Artemus Jones, which stated: "There is Artemus Jones with a woman who is not his wife, who must be, you know – the other thing!" The "real" Artemus Jones, a practising barrister, brought an action for defamation. It was held that even though the article was intended to be humorous, it was capable of adversely affecting the reputation of the plaintiff and was therefore defamatory. Evidence was accepted that a number of friends and acquaintances of the plaintiff had read the article and had understood it to refer to the plaintiff.

8.3.4 Reference to a class

Whether a member of a class of persons can bring an action for defamation will depend on the size of the class and the generality of the statement made. The plaintiff must show that he has been specifically identified. In *Le Fanu v. Malcolmson* (1848), an article about the alleged cruelties practised upon employees by Irish factory owners was deemed to be defamatory at the suit of the plaintiff, a factory owner from Waterford, due to the inclusion of certain statements in the article which allowed him to be identified specifically.

8.4 Defences to an action for defamation

As stated above, the law of defamation attempts to strike a balance between the competing rights to reputation and free expression. The law attempts to fulfil the aim of protecting reputation by allowing an action to be brought against the publisher of a defamatory statement. There are, however, a number of defences, which a defendant can raise in response to an action in defamation. In this way, every citizen's right to free expression is vindicated under Irish law.

8.4.1 Justification

Truth is always a complete defence to an allegation of defamation. The existence of this defence is justified on the basis that the law will not protect a reputation built on lies. However, contrary to the general rule that it is for the plaintiff to prove every element of his case, under Irish law the onus of proof in defamation actions shifts to the publisher who raises the defence of justification, to establish the veracity of the statement. The reversal of the onus of proof places a heavy burden on defendants and may be contrasted with decisions in the United States such as *Philadelphia Newspapers Inc. v. Hepps* (1986). In this case, the defendants published a series of newspaper articles alleging that the plaintiff had links to organised crime and that these links were used to influence the State's governmental processes. The defendants appealed the decision of the Philadelphia Supreme Court, which had held that the onus of proving the truth of the statement rested with the publisher. The U.S. Supreme Court reversed the lower court's decision and held that the onus remained on the plaintiff to prove every element of the charge. It is highly unlikely that such a position could be adopted in

Ireland due to the constitutional protection granted to the citizen's right to a good name under article 40.3.2°.

The defence of justification will succeed if the gist of the statement is true, even though certain details may not be accurate. In *Alexander v. North Eastern Railway Co.* (1865), a inaccurate statement was published which alleged that the plaintiff was convicted of travelling on one of the defendant's trains without a ticket and was consequently fined £1 and sentenced to three weeks' imprisonment. In fact, the plaintiff had been fined £1 and had been imprisoned for two weeks. The Court found that the statement was true in substance and the part that was not true did not distort the general tenor of the statement. This case can be contrasted with that of *Crawford v. Todd* (1941), where it was claimed that the plaintiff operated a gambling den and sold liquor without a licence. The latter allegation proved to be untrue, giving rise to a successful action in defamation. The extent of the inaccuracy nullified the defence. This aspect of Irish defamation law has been subject to statutory intervention in the form of section 22 of the Defamation Act 1961. Under section 22, where two or more allegations are made, the fact that one is not true will not render the defence of justification void by reason only that the truth of every charge is not proved, if the words not proved to be true do not materially injure the plaintiff's reputation having regard to the truth of the remaining charges.

In *Cooper-Flynn v. RTÉ* (2000), it was alleged in a television programme that the plaintiff advised and encouraged clients to purchase investment portfolios for the purpose of evading tax. The defendants pleaded justification in response to the plaintiff's claim. The jury found that the allegations made by the third-named defendant in the programme were untrue. However, the jury did accept the veracity of allegations (repeated by the second-named defendant on the programme) that the plaintiff had induced others to partake in the investment scheme. The jury decided that the allegations made by the third-named defendant (in light of the allegations that had been proven to be true) did not materially damage the plaintiff's reputation and the defence of justification was successful.

8.4.2 Privilege

The law recognises that on some occasions an individual's right to free expression should not be inhibited. Where a potentially defamatory statement is made on such an occasion, the maker of the statement will be granted immunity from an action in defamation. In those circumstances, the statement or occasion is privileged. Public policy dictates that the recipient's "right to know" outweighs the individual's right to a good name in such circumstances.

There are two forms of privilege in Irish law: absolute privilege and qualified privilege.

8.4.2.1 Absolute privilege

This is an absolute privilege in the sense that it protects all statements made in a particular context, regardless of motive.

(a) Presidential privilege: This is constitutional in origin. Article 13.8.1° of the Constitution provides that the President is not answerable to any court for the exercise and performance of the powers and functions of his or her office, or for any act done or purporting to be done by his or her in the exercise and performance of these powers and functions. This immunity would appear without question to embrace defamatory statements made by the President, though not, of course, those made by the President outside the contexts specified by Article 13.8.1°.

(b) Parliamentary privilege: Like presidential privilege, the present form of parliamentary privilege is constitutional in origin (Articles 15.12 and 15.13). This privilege includes all official reports, publications and utterances in either House of the Oireachtas. Members of the House are not amenable to any court in respect of utterances in either House. In *A.G. v. Hamilton (No. 2)* (1993), the Supreme Court held that Article 15 provides far more than a mere defence in respect of a claim for defamation; that the Court has no jurisdiction to deal with the matter at all; and that members are only answerable for utterances made in the Houses to the Houses themselves. A member of a House can be deemed to have waived the parliamentary privilege, however, where he repeats the statement outside the House in a manner which is "voluntary, conscious and deliberate."

A majority of the Supreme Court in *A.G. v. Hamilton (No. 2)* acknowledged that if the immunity were removed, utterances in the Houses would be likely to provoke a variety of legal proceedings – and therefore the word "privilege" in the Constitution should not be construed narrowly. It was further held that Article 15 has the effect that any utterance in either House cannot be the subject matter of any legal proceedings, wheresoever published. (Denham J. dissented on this point, ruling that the protection under Article 15 is limited to statements made in the House and does not include repetition elsewhere.)

(c) Newspaper and broadcast reports of court proceedings: Section 18(1) of the 1961 Act gives a privilege to "fair and accurate", reports in newspapers or broadcasts of contemporaneous court proceedings – so that where the report is on balance "fair and accurate" the publisher will not be liable for inaccuracies and slips. In *Lynam v. Gowning* (1880), the privilege was deemed not to extend to reported statements made in court when the legal proceedings are over, such as a bystander's spontaneous statement in the courtroom accusing a witness of perjury.

(d) Judicial proceedings: All statements made in the course of judicial proceedings, and documents made in contemplation of proceedings, are privileged. In *Kennedy v. Hilliard* (1859), the Court held that this immunity is based on public policy so anyone can speak freely in court without being influenced by fear of defamation. In *Re Haughey* (1971), the Supreme Court held that a witness who takes advantage of his position as a witness to utter something defamatory which has no bearing on the matter before the court may lose the immunity, and the defamation may become actionable. Tribunal proceedings also benefit from the privilege when exercising the function of a court, *e.g.* a disciplinary committee of the Law Society or military court-martial proceedings, but it does not extend to bodies acting in an administrative as opposed to a legal/judicial capacity.

(e) State communication: Absolute privilege is conferred on the legislative, judicial, and executive branches of government and the communications between them.

(f) Communication between husband and wife: This point features earlier in the chapter as the rule that when statements are exchanged between husband and wife, there is no "publication" and therefore no defamation. It is otherwise reasoned – since the end result is the same – that the law absolutely privileges communications passing between husband and wife, and that it does so "to guard with special care the institution of marriage" (as constitutionally obliged to do so by Article 41.3.1°).

8.4.2.2 Qualified privilege

In certain situations, a person may have a duty to speak to others who have a reciprocal interest in receiving that information. Where such statements are made without malice, they may be considered privileged in a qualified sense and the maker is immune from a defamation suit.

(a) Duty or interest: In order to establish whether the privilege arises in any particular situation, the maker must establish that he had a duty or interest to make the statement to the party concerned. According to Lord Atkinson in *Adam v. Ward* (1917), this duty may be of a "legal, social, or moral" nature. In *Kirkwood Hackett v. Tierney* (1952), the President of UCD questioned a student, in the presence of the College Bursar, regarding a money draft which had been paid out in error. It was held that the President was not liable in defamation as he was under a duty to make a full enquiry in respect of the money draft and therefore his communications were privileged.

Similarly, in the recent judgment of the English High Court in *Kearns & Co. v. General Council of the Bar* (2002), the defence of qualified privilege was successfully pleaded. In that case, the Bar Council received a letter from a barrister expressing concern about instructions that junior barristers in his chambers were receiving from a company known as Kearns Agency. The barrister was of the view that the activities of the company may have been in breach of the Bar's code of conduct. After considering the matter, the Bar Council issued a circular to the heads of chambers and to senior clerks to the effect that Kearns & Co. was not a firm of solicitors and that it would not be proper for barristers to accept instructions from Kearns Agency. It transpired that this information was incorrect. The plaintiffs were indeed a firm of solicitors and, furthermore, Kearns Agency was a body recognised by the Law Society and was able to instruct counsel. Once the error came to light, the Bar Council offered a correction and apology. The plaintiff brought an action in defamation. The High Court found that the defence of qualified privilege protected the defendant's statements. Eady J. found that the Bar Council was under a duty to communicate the information to its members and in the absence of malice was protected from an action in defamation.

Qualified privilege may also be granted in circumstances where the maker of the statement is under an obligation to protect an interest. The interests which are deemed worthy of protection are not closed. In *Denvir v. Taylor* (1936), a report by a supervisor relating to the conduct of an employee was deemed privileged.

It is important to note that in all situations where qualified privilege is successfully pleaded, the person or persons to whom the statement is made must have a reciprocal interest in receiving the information. Thus, the College Bursar in *Kirkwood Hackett v. Tierney* had an interest in the investigation conducted by the College President. Similarly, in *Hartery v. Welltrade (Middle East) Ltd* (1978), a complaint made to a member of the Garda Síochána was considered privileged.

(b) Malice: Qualified privilege will not attach to statements made with malice. Brett L.J. had stated in *Clark v. Molyneux* (1877) that:

> If the occasion is privileged it is so for some reason, and the defendant is only entitled to the protection of the privilege if he uses the occasion for that reason. He is not entitled to the protection if he uses the occasion for some indirect and wrong motive. If he uses the occasion to gratify his anger or his malice, he uses the occasion not for the reason which makes the occasion privileged, but for an indirect and wrong motive.

Malice exists where the maker of the statement did not honestly believe that what he stated was true or where he was reckless as to whether it was true or not. In *Horrocks v. Lowe* (1974), Lord Diplock examined the elements necessary for establishing malice:

> If it be proved that he did not believe that what he published was true this is generally conclusive evidence of express malice, for no sense of duty or desire to protect his own legitimate interests can justify a man in telling deliberate and injurious falsehoods about another ... what is required on the part of the defamer to entitle him to the protection of the privilege is positive belief in the truth of what he published ... If he publishes untrue defamatory matter recklessly, without considering or caring whether it be true or not, he is in this, as in other branches of the law, treated as if he knew it to be false.

Possession of an honest belief in the statement made is central. Evidence that the maker of the statement did not possess such a belief may be established by extrinsic facts, such as personal animosity between the parties.

8.4.2.3 The extension of qualified privilege

The question as to whether statements published by the media should attract the protection of qualified privilege has generated much judicial and academic debate. In *New York Times v. Sullivan* (1964), the U.S. Supreme Court held that the plaintiff, a public official, could not succeed in an action for defamation against the defendant newspaper which had criticised his conduct as Police Commissioner, unless it could be proven that such criticism was motivated by malice. Brennan J. explained the Court's decision as follows:

> A rule compelling the critic of official conduct to guarantee the truth of all his factual assertions – and to do so on pain of libel judgments virtually unlimited in amount – leads to a comparable "self-censorship". Allowance of the defence of truth, with the burden of proving it

on the defendant, does not mean that only false speech will be deterred … Under such a rule, would-be critics of official conduct may be deterred from voicing their criticism, even though it is believed to be true and even though it is in fact true, because of doubt whether it can be proved in court or fear of the expense of having to do so.

The question as to whether the defence should be extended in this manner also arose in the English case of *Reynolds v. Times Newspapers Ltd* (1999). In that case, the defendant published an article about the plaintiff, a former Taoiseach, under the heading "Goodbye Gombeen man." The general tenor of the article was that the plaintiff had deliberately and dishonestly misled the Dáil. The defendant argued that the article should come within the ambit of a generic qualified privilege protecting "political information." The defendant submitted that it was under a duty to publish such information and that the general public had a corresponding interest in receiving the information. The House of Lords rejected the argument that political information such as that contained in the offending article should be granted any such protection. Lord Nicholls was of the view that the introduction of such a concept would not provide adequate protection for the reputation of the individual. He pointed out that if "political information" was to be protected by qualified privilege, the plaintiff could only succeed in bringing an action for defamation if he could establish that the statement was motivated by malice. Establishing malice in this context would prove highly onerous, particularly in light of the fact that newspapers in the U.K. were not under an obligation to divulge their sources.

Whilst the House of Lords did not approve of the creation of a generic qualified privilege regarding political information, Lord Nicholls did recognise the importance of the media's right to free expression. His Lordship was of the view that the publication by the media of a defamatory article could be protected by qualified privilege in certain circumstances. Thus, it would now appear that if the publication is the result of reasonable and responsible journalism, it will attract the privilege. In order to determine whether the publisher acted in such a manner, Lord Nicholls stated that account should be taken of the following factors:

(1) The seriousness of the allegation. The more serious the charge, the more the public is misinformed and the individual harmed, if the allegation is not true. (2) The nature of the information, and the extent to which the subject matter is a matter of public concern. (3) The source of the information. Some informants have no direct knowledge of the

events. Some have their own axes to grind, or are being paid for their stories. (4) The steps taken to verify the information. (5) The status of the information. The allegation may have already been the subject of an investigation which commands respect. (6) The urgency of the matter. News is often a perishable commodity. (7) Whether comment was sought from the plaintiff. He may have information others do not possess or have not disclosed ... (8) Whether the article contained the gist of the plaintiff's side of the story. (9) The tone of the article. A newspaper can raise queries or call for an investigation. It need not adopt allegations as statements of fact. (10) The circumstances of the publication, including the timing. The list is not exhaustive. The weight to be given to these and any other relevant factors will vary from case to case.

Lord Nicholls offered the proponents of press freedom further encouragement in the following passage from his judgment:

In general, a newspaper's unwillingness to disclose the identity of its sources should not weigh against it. Further, it should always be remembered that journalists act without the benefit of the clear light of hindsight. Matters which are obvious in retrospect may have been far from clear in the heat of the moment. Above all, the court should have particular regard to the importance of freedom of expression. The press discharges vital functions as a bloodhound as well as watchdog. The court should be slow to conclude that a publication was not in the public interest and, therefore, the public had no right to know, especially when the information is in the field of political discussion. Any lingering doubts should be resolved in favour of publication.

Despite the emphatic rejection of the generic qualified privilege defence, the judgment of Lord Nicholls did recognise the importance of a free press. Qualified privilege has been pleaded in a number of English cases since *Reynolds* with varying degrees of success.

In *Grobbelaar v. News Group Newspapers Ltd* (2001), the plaintiff was a well-known professional footballer. The defendant published a series of articles alleging that the plaintiff had taken bribes in order to "fix" football matches. The allegations were based on a video-tape "sting" arranged by the defendant, in which it was alleged that the plaintiff had admitted to the offences. In the High Court, the jury awarded the plaintiff £85,000 in damages. This decision was appealed to the Court of Appeal, where it was held that the articles did not give rise to an occasion that could be protected by qualified privilege. However, the Court of Appeal, quashing the verdict of the jury in the High

Court, found that the defendant had successfully invoked the defence of substantial justification.

This determination was successfully appealed to the House of Lords, where the plaintiff's argument that the sting of the libel "lay in the allegation that he had deliberately fixed or 'thrown' matches and was prepared to do so again," and not in the statement that he had taken bribes. The truth of the former allegation he contended, had not been proven and could not therefore give rise to the defence of justification. Their Lordships agreed and the decision of the Court of Appeal was overturned; however, the plaintiff was only awarded the derisory sum of £1 in damages.

The question of qualified privilege was dealt with by the Court of Appeal, which held, utilising the 10 steps devised by Lord Nicholls in *Reynolds,* that the articles were not occasions which should be protected by qualified privilege. In particular, it was the view of the Court that the exposé did not contain the plaintiff's side of the story and that the timing and tone of the article were designed to suit the defendant's interests. In reaching its judgment, the Court of Appeal emphasised the importance of investigative journalism in modern society:

> Investigative journalism can be of considerable public benefit, but without the incentive of being in a position to publish an exclusive story on a sensational subject a newspaper will inevitably be less enthusiastic about committing its time and resources to investigating the story. The prospect of the resulting "scoop" seems to me to be part and parcel of the process of investigative journalism.

Qualified privilege was pleaded successfully in *GKR Karate (U.K.) Ltd v. Porch* (2000). In that case, the defendants published an article which alleged, *inter alia*, that the plaintiffs were "doorstep salesmen flogging dodgy karate lessons" and that the instructors they used to deliver these lessons were recruited from job centres or newspaper adverts and had a minimal knowledge of karate. The Court explained its reasoning in finding that the newspaper article was privileged in the following terms:

> A privileged occasion exists if the public is entitled to know the particular information. That is, if it was the journalist's social or moral duty to communicate it and the interest of the particular public to receive it. This is determined in the light of all the circumstances of the publication and, and in particular, whether the sources were, or appeared to be reliable to a reasonable and responsible journalist. While Lord Nicholls' ten examples are not to be taken as written in

stone, they form the basic framework upon which a judge can do the balancing exercise.

It would appear that the decision in *Reynolds* has liberalised the law on defamation in the U.K. A publisher may now escape liability for publishing a defamatory statement if he can show he acted reasonably, responsibly and in good faith at all times in relation to its publication, notwithstanding the fact that the offending publication may have been false and defamatory.

8.4.3 Offer of amends

Section 21 of the 1961 Act provides a defence to someone who innocently (and not unreasonably) published a defamatory statement and who then went on to make an offer of amends for doing so. An offer of amends will, pursuant to section 21, include the correction of the words complained of, an apology to the aggrieved party, and, where copies of a document have been distributed, the taking of such steps as are practicable to notify persons to whom copies have been distributed. On accepting the offer of amends, the plaintiff will effectively have brought an end to the threatened action. If the offer is rejected, however, the offer of amends will be a complete defence if it has been made as soon as practicable after the defendant became aware of the potential defamation. To be effective, the offer of amends must be expressed to be made for the purposes of section 21, and it must be accompanied by an affidavit of the facts relied upon to show the defendant's innocence.

8.4.4 Consent

The general defence of *volenti non fit injuria* applies in relation to defamation as it does in other areas of tort law. Section 34(1)(b) of the Civil Liability Act 1961 provides that a plaintiff cannot complain if he has "agreed to waive his legal rights ... whether or not for value." In *O'Hanlon v. ESB* (1969), it was held that "agreement" for these purposes requires a specific, clearly understood waiver to recovery for the injury in question.

8.4.5 Fair comment on matters of public interest

The defence of fair comment provides further protection for free expression. In order to plead fair comment, the publisher must establish that the comment was made in relation to a matter of public interest, that what was said was comment and not a statement of fact, and that the comment was fair, in other words, it was honest.

8.4.5.1 Public interest

The statement must be made on a matter of public interest. Matters of public interest in this context include matters relating to the government and the administration of the State, as well as matters of literary or artistic or similar nature submitted to the public for approval.

In *London Artists v. Littler* (1969), Lord Denning stated that:

> Whenever a matter is such as to affect people at large, so that they may be legitimately interested in, or concerned at, what is going on; or what may happen to them or others; then it is a matter of public interest on which everyone is entitled to make fair comment.

The defence allows an individual to comment critically on those matters which are considered to be in the public interest, without fear of being sued for defamation.

8.4.5.2 Comment as opposed to fact

The comment must be a view honestly held and based on established and proven facts. It is important, although sometimes by no means straightforward, to distinguish comment from fact. Facts must be proved to be true (or privileged), while comment must only be shown to be fair or honest. In *Dakhyl v. Labouchere* (1908), the plaintiff described himself as "a specialist in the treatment of deafness, ear, nose and throat diseases." The defendant, however, referred to him as "a quack of the rankest species." It was held that the defendant's statement was an expression of opinion, not a statement of fact and was therefore covered by the defence.

8.4.5.3 Comment must be fair

The statement must be fair in the sense that it must be the honestly held view of the maker. Therefore a subjective test is applied. In *Campbell v. Spottiswoode* (1863), the defendant's comment consisted of an allegation that the plaintiff's purpose behind starting a scheme to spread Christianity amongst the Chinese was to promote the sale of his own newspaper. It was held that although the defendant honestly believed that what he had said was true, he was not entitled to rely on the defence of fair comment because there was no reasonable basis of fact for his allegation. The "comment must be relevant to the facts to which it is addressed. It cannot be used as a cloak for mere invective."

8.4.6 Apology

The law of defamation does not recognise a general defence based on apology or offer of apology. Such evidence may, however, be relevant in mitigation of damages by virtue of section 17 of the 1961 Act which requires that the apology be made before the commencement of the proceedings, or reasonably soon afterwards.

Further reading

McMahon & Binchy, *Law of Torts* (Butterworths, 2000), pp. 879, 966; Quill, *Torts in Ireland* (Gill & Macmillan, 1999), pp. 287–319; Fleming, *The Law of Torts* (LBC, 1998), pp. 580–663; O'Dell, "Does Defamation Value Free Expression? The Possible Influence of *New York Times v. Sullivan* on Irish Law" (1990) 12 D.U.L.J. (ns) 50.

9. NUISANCE

9.1 Introduction

The tort of nuisance encompasses a range of conduct so wide as to almost defy definition. It links the emission of offensive smells, the making of hoax bomb warnings, excessive noise, cockroach infestation, pigeon droppings, vibrations causing structural damage to property, and the keeping of a house of ill-repute. The tort's particular usefulness is in the arbitration of conflicts between competing uses of land.

> Nuisance in tort law consists essentially of the unreasonable interference with another person in the exercise of his or her rights generally associated with the occupation of property. The action traces its origins to medieval times, yet it displays a continuing vitality, being capable of adjustment to contemporary notions of ecological balance and the control of pollution. (McMahon & Binchy, 2000, p. 675)

Traditionally, nuisance was regarded as being particularly special in the way it focused on the harm to the plaintiff, rather than the nature of the conduct of the defendant who caused it. For example, in *Sampson v. Hodson-Pressinger* (1981), the defendant was held liable in nuisance for the ordinary use of his property, the tiled terrace in a converted flat, which due to its faulty construction created excessive noise on adjacent properties. However, it is likely that this plaintiff-centred approach will not survive the House of Lords' most recent pronouncement on the point in *Baxter v. Camden London Borough Council* (1999), where, in similar circumstances, particular emphasis was placed on the importance of balancing competing interests rather than the nature of the injury suffered by the plaintiff. Lord Millett characterised the plaintiff's case in the following terms:

> I do not wish to be thought indifferent to Miss Baxter's plight. I have the greatest sympathy for her. But the fact remains that she took a flat on the first floor of a house, knowing that the ground and second floors were also occupied as residential flats, and expecting their occupants to live normal lives. This is all that they are doing. She has no cause to complain of their activities, which mirror her own; or of the council for having permitted them by letting the adjoining flats. Her real complaint is, and always has been, of the absence of ade-

quate sound insulation. Her complaint, however well founded, cannot be redressed by the law of tort; any remedy must lie in statute or contract.

Actionable nuisance may be public or private in nature. Public nuisance is concerned with the infringement of rights enjoyed by members of the public and not with the enjoyment of private property. It is only actionable on proof of particular damage. The key characteristic of private nuisance is the affixing of liability on someone pursuant to an act or omission which causes annoyance, prejudice or disturbance to another in the enjoyment of land. Such disturbance may take the form of physical damage to the land or, more usually, an interference with the occupier's reasonable enjoyment of it.

Whilst there was an initial tendency to limit the ambit of nuisance to interferences with occupiers' enjoyment of their property, in the nineteenth century the courts displayed a greater willingness to treat conduct causing physical or structural damage as nuisance. This development greatly increased the importance of the tort. However, by the twentieth century, wrongful acts causing property damage were predominantly considered within the rubric of the tort of negligence, and in this way the development of negligence served to diminish the importance of the tort of nuisance. Whilst a plaintiff might claim for physical damage to his land under both torts, in such cases "talk of nuisance is at most added as mere surplusage" (Fleming, 1998, p.458). Indeed, in his article *The Place of Private Nuisance in the Modern Law of Torts* (1989 C.L.J. 214), Conor Gearty suggests that claims in respect of physical damage to land should be excluded from the tort of nuisance altogether. The practical significance of maintaining such a distinction lies in the fact that in cases of nuisance causing physical damage to property, unlawful use is presumed (*St. Helen's Smelting Co. v. Tipping* (1865), *Video London Sound Studio Ltd v. Asticus Ltd* (2001)).

Private nuisance is a land-based tort. It protects rights in, and holds a defendant liable for unreasonable conduct carried out on, land. The requirement that the impugned conduct be in some way associated with land or an interest therein was reinforced by the House of Lords in the recent decision of *Hunter v. Canary Wharf* (1997) where Lord Hoffmann stated that:

> once it is understood that nuisances "productive of sensible personal discomfort" do not constitute a separate tort of causing discomfort to people but are merely part of a single tort of causing injury to land,

the rule the plaintiff must have an interest in the land falls into place as logical and, indeed, inevitable.

This decision will receive further consideration in 9.2.5 below.

9.2 Private nuisance

A private nuisance is created where the plaintiff is adversely affected in his enjoyment of land or some right or interest in land. Private nuisance consists of either the wrongful interference with the physical integrity of the plaintiff's property, or the wrongful interference with the plaintiff's reasonable enjoyment of his property.

The tort of private nuisance is not actionable *per se*. Actual damage must be proved. However, there are three exceptions to this general rule. In the first instance, the court may presume the existence of damage where none is proved if to require such evidence would be superfluous. Further, no damage need be established by a plaintiff seeking damages for interference with an easement or *profit á prendre*. Finally, an injunction may be granted in a *quia timet* action (where harm is reasonably feared to be imminent, but has not yet occurred).

9.2.1 The question of reasonableness

The concept of reasonableness is the central theme in the tort of nuisance. In *Hanrahan v. Merck Sharpe & Dohme* (1988), Henchy J. (in the Supreme Court) commented:

> It is clear from the authorities on the law of nuisance that what an occupier of land is entitled to as against his neighbour is the comfortable and healthy enjoyment of the land to the degree that would be expected by an ordinary person whose requirements are reasonable in all the circumstances.

The reasonableness of the defendant's conduct is judged "according to the ordinary usages of mankind living in a particular society," (per Lord Wright in *Sedleigh-Denfield v. O'Callaghan* (1940)). However, reasonableness for the purposes of the tort of nuisance is distinct from its use in negligence. The issue of reasonableness is approached by attempting to balance the competing rights of neighbours, it is a process of compromise, a "rule of give and take, of live and let live" (*Bamford v. Turnley* (1862)).

A commonsense approach is adopted by the courts based on what it is reasonable to expect between neighbours. The courts first examine the *utility* of the defendant's conduct, and secondly the *gravity of the harm* resulting from it. In nuisance, the court is especially concerned to balance the competing interests of plaintiffs and defendants. Allowances will be made for the social and economic context in which the alleged infringement has taking place. For example, the running of commercial premises in a mixed (*i.e.* commercial and residential) area will necessarily involve a likelihood of some degree of personal discomfort for neighbouring property owners. In the words of Thesiger L.J. (in *Sturges v. Bridgman* (1879)), "what would be a nuisance in Belgrave Square would not necessarily be so in Bermondsey." Similarly, Tuckey L.J. in the Court of Appeal's decision in *Baxter v. Camden London Borough Council* observed that:

> In the case of noise nuisance ... the court will obviously have to consider the locality, age and physical characteristics of the premises in question. Occupiers of low-cost, high density housing must be expected to tolerate higher levels of noise from their neighbours than others in more substantial and spacious premises.

In *O'Kane v. Campbell* (1985), the defendant's shop was located on the corner of North Circular Road (a primarily commercial area) and Glengariff Parade (which was almost completely residential). The defendants commenced trading as a 24-hour shop, which caused disturbance to the plaintiff, who lived on Glengariff Parade, in the early hours of the morning. The court noted that the noise was the inevitable result of persons using the shop throughout the night. Lynch J. noted that if the shop had been located wholly on Glengarriff Parade, it would have amounted to a clear and actionable nuisance on account of the traffic congestion and noise caused. If the shop was wholly located on the North Circular Road, he doubted whether any actionable nuisance would have occurred. In recognition of the opposing interests of the parties, he made an order restraining the defendants from trading between midnight and 6 a.m. In the recent decision of O'Sullivan J. in *Molumby v. Kearns* (1999), the alleged acts of nuisance were carried out in a mainly residential area "adjoining a busy road in front and with an industrial estate, authorised by appropriate planning, in its midst." The learned trial judge stated:

> I do not think that the fact that the residences immediately adjoin the industrial estate means that the estate must close down. I do not think this would be reasonable. Equally, I do not think that the noise, fumes and general activity and traffic movements on the estate should be such as to cause an undue impact on the amenities of the nearby residences.

The learned trial judge concluded that the plaintiffs had not been afforded "the comfortable and healthy enjoyment" of their property on the basis set out by Henchy J. in *Hanrahan*. For this reason, he made an order that:

> ... the gates should remain closed except between 8.15 am and 6.15 pm Mondays to Fridays and 9 am and 1 pm on Saturdays. No commercial vehicles should be permitted access to the estate when the gates are closed. I consider, however, that the Defendants should be entitled to park up to three private vehicles in the estate outside opening hours to facilitate senior employees working late. There should be a large clear notice at the entrance of the estate limiting speed to 8 miles an hour and prohibiting the running of engines during loading and unloading. No fork-lift or pallet trucks should be used on the estate other than electric or battery operated units with rubber wheels.

What amounts to reasonableness is dependent not only on the location of the impugned act, but also on the social conditions within which the act occurred. So, in *Bridlington Relay v. Yorkshire Electricity Board* (1965), it was held that "the ability to receive television free from occasional ... electrical interference is not so important a part of an ordinary householder's enjoyment of his property that it ought to be protected under the tort of nuisance." Salmond notes (1992, at p. 62) that "it may be doubted whether this view represents the law [today]."

On the general issue of the reasonableness of the defendant's behaviour, the English case *Christie v. Davey* (1893) clearly illustrates the way the defendant's malice will transform what would otherwise be a reasonable use of his land into an actionable nuisance. The plaintiff, a music teacher, delivered about 17 hours of music lessons per week in her house. Her property was separated from the defendant's by a party wall. The defendant, exasperated by the noise from the music lessons given up to a late hour by the plaintiff, attempted by a clumsily written letter to have the noise discontinued. When this failed, he resorted to playing instruments, blowing whistles, knocking on trays and making other noise in "mock concerts" designed to annoy the plaintiff. The defendant was held to have committed a nuisance. North J. stated "if what has taken place occurred between two sets of persons both perfectly innocent, I should have taken an entirely different view of the case." In this context, Salmond & Heuston (1992, at pp. 65–66) note that:

> [t]he concept of "reasonableness" for the purposes of the principles relating to unreasonable interference in the law of nuisance, may have to be understood in a subjective as well as an objective sense. There-

fore if acts otherwise justified on the ground of reciprocity between neighbours are done wantonly or maliciously the defendant cannot argue that, *e.g.* the volume of noise created could, from some abstract viewpoint, be regarded as within the limits of what the plaintiff ought to be expected to tolerate.

Hollywood Silver Fox Farm Ltd v. Emmett (1936) also illustrates the effect of malice on the part of the defendant. Damages and an injunction were granted when the defendant ordered his son to fire guns on his own land as near as possible to the plaintiff's breeding pens in order that the latter's vixen might refuse to breed or miscarry, although clearly he was entitled to shoot on his own land for pleasure or to control the rabbit population.

9.2.2 It is no defence that the plaintiff came to the nuisance

It is irrelevant that the defendant has carried on the impugned acts for many years without complaint, and that the plaintiff had full knowledge of those acts when moving on to the land on which he now claims to have suffered the nuisance. The fundamental test of *unreasonable interference* remains that laid down by Thesiger L.J. in *Sturges v. Bridgman* (1879). Here, a confectioner had, for more than 20 years, used heavy machinery on his premises, which abutted on the garden of a physician. However the noise and vibration did not disturb the plaintiff and were not complained of until, in 1873, the plaintiff erected a consulting-room at the end of his garden. At this point the noise and vibration became a nuisance to him and he successfully brought an action for an injunction to restrain the defendant's unreasonable behaviour. Similarly, in *Bliss v. Hall* (1838), the defendant argued that his candle-making business, which caused fumes and offensive smells, had pre-dated the plaintiff's arrival by three years. The Court held that this was no defence to the plaintiff's action in nuisance. However, this principle does not extend to claims taken by tenants against their landlords. A tenant is deemed to take the property subject to any nuisances emanating from other premises prior to the creation of the tenancy. (See the Court of Appeal's decision in *Baxter v. Camden London Borough Council*. This point was not addressed by the House of Lords on appeal.) Of course, this exception in no way precludes the tenant's independent right of action in nuisance against the creator of the nuisance.

9.2.3 Public convenience

There is a clear divergence of judicial opinion on whether courts should take into account public convenience in ascertaining the reasonableness of a defendant's conduct. Maguire C.J. expressed a negative opinion in *Bellew v. Cement Ltd* (1946). Here the defendant asked the Court to consider the shortage of cement following World War II (a shortage which was being alleviated by the acts alleged to constitute a nuisance against the plaintiff) as a factor to be considered in determining the reasonableness of the defendant's behaviour. The Supreme Court refused to take public convenience into account when determining the rights of private parties. This is clearly at variance with decisions such as *Andreae v. Selfridge* (1938) and *Clifford v. Drug Treatment Centre Board* (1997). The latter cases represent a more civic-minded approach taken by the courts, whereby regard is had to society's needs as well as the plaintiff's. In *Clifford*, McCracken J. refused to grant the injunction sought by the plaintiff, which would have required the defendant to reduce the number of drug addicts treated at its premises, but did prohibit the defendant from increasing beyond existing levels the number of patients treated. In *Andreae v. Selfridge*, the Court of Appeal varied the order of Bennett J. at first instance in holding that:

> ... no cause of action arises in respect of operations, such as demolition and building, if they are reasonably carried on and all reasonable and proper steps are taken to ensure that no undue inconvenience is caused to neighbours. In determining what is reasonable, methods of building and demolition must not be taken as stabilized, but new inventions and new methods may be reasonable in the altered circumstances and developments of the day ... the evidence showed that the plaintiff was inconvenienced by the dust and noise, but in estimating the damages the Court must be careful not to penalize the defendant company by throwing into the scales against it losses caused by operations which the defendant company was legitimately entitled to carry out; the defendant company could be made liable only in respect of matters in which it crossed the permissible line.

The order of Bennett J. was varied by reducing the damages awarded from £4,500 to £1,000.

9.2.4 The position of the sensitive user

As a general rule, no action will lie for nuisance in respect of damage which is due solely to the fact that the plaintiff is abnormally sensitive to interference. In the words of Lord Robertson in *Eastern and South African Telegraph Co. v. Cape Town Tramways* (1902), "a man cannot increase the liabilities of his neighbour by applying his own property to special uses, whether for business or pleasure." In this case, the Privy Council dismissed the plaintiff's claim in nuisance for electrical interference with the transmission of messages via an underwater cable. Similarly, in *Robinson v. Kilvert* (1889), where the defendant's pipes heated and thereby damaged the plaintiff's stock of brown paper, which was characterised as "an exceptionally delicate trade", it was held that no nuisance had been caused, since the heat from the pipes would not have prejudicially affected any ordinary trade.

It is important to distinguish between the effect of abnormal sensitivity before and after the nuisance has been established. Once an actionable nuisance has been established, the law will intervene to protect abnormally delicate and sensitive operations. So, in *McKinnon Industries v. Walker* (1951), the plaintiff's enjoyment of his property (from which he operated a commercial nursery) was impaired by the emission of fumes and sulphur dioxide gas from the defendant's factory. The Privy Council rejected the defendant's argument that, even if an injunction were granted, it should be modified so as to exclude protection for the plaintiff's orchids, the growing of which was a "delicate operation". Once the plaintiff's ordinary enjoyment was affected, there was no reason to treat damage to orchids differently from damage to any other flower, plant or shrub.

9.2.5 Who may sue in nuisance?

The general rule is that landowners and occupiers may sue in nuisance. Two Irish cases confirm that an occupier may take an action in nuisance, *Halpin v. Tara Mines* (Gannon J., 1976) and *Hanrahan v. Merck Sharpe & Dohme* (Henchy J., 1988).

In *Motherwell v. Motherwell* (1976), the Alberta Supreme Court went further and held that a person with a right of residence may also maintain an action in nuisance in relation to the land (in this case the nuisance consisted of the making of "crank" telephone calls). However, in *Hunter v. Canary Wharf Ltd* (1997), the House of Lords refused to permit a mere licensee (*i.e.* one who did not enjoy exclusive possession) to maintain an action in nuisance in respect of interruption to his television signal caused by the erection of the defendant's skyscraper. In a similar vein, in *Malone v. Laskey* (1907, Court of Appeal), the occupier's wife who suffered injury when a bracket fell from a wall, allegedly caused by vibrations coming from next door, was precluded from suing in private nuisance since she had no interest in the premises and was a mere licensee. The strictness of this approach may be ameliorated somewhat by the observation of Lord Hoffman in *Hunter* that:

> [t]he courts today will readily assume that a wife has acquired a beneficial interest in the matrimonial home. If so, she will be entitled to sue for damage to that interest.

It seems that Irish courts have not been persuaded to adopt this more restrictive approach to who may sue in nuisance. In *Royal Dublin Society v. Yates* (1997), Shanley J. in the High Court cited the Supreme Court's decision in *Hanrahan v. Merck Sharpe & Dohme* to support the taking of "a different and more flexible approach" to the question in this jurisdiction. Further evidence of the Irish courts' flexibility in this regard is provided by O'Sullivan J.'s decision in *Molumby v. Kearns* (1999). Commenting on this decision, McMahon & Binchy (2000) note that:

> O'Sullivan J's preference for a test based on the plaintiffs being the "occupier of the land", with no necessity to establish a legal interest over and above this, clearly intended this to be broader than the *Hunter* approach; precisely how much broader is not entirely clear. The concept of occupier is a somewhat elastic one, dependant on the particular context.

In *Pemberton v. Southwark London Borough Council* (2000), the Court accepted the plaintiff's entitlement to maintain an action notwithstanding her status as a "tolerated trespasser." The defendant council granted the appellant a secure tenancy of a flat. Following the plaintiff's failure to discharge her arrears of rent, the defendant sought and obtained an order for possession of the demised premises, not to be enforced for 28 days, in any event, and for so long as the plaintiff punctually paid instalments of the arrears in addition to the current rent. On the plaintiff's failure to pay these instalments she became a "tolerated trespasser" and was liable to be evicted on the issue and execution of a warrant of possession. The plaintiff subsequently issued proceedings in nuisance against the council in respect of an infestation of cockroaches. The council defended her claim by arguing that she had no cause of action since she was no longer a tenant. On appeal to the

Court of Appeal, it was held that a tolerated trespasser has the exclusive right to occupy premises for the period she remains thereon. It was noted that while the order for possession ends the contractual relationship between the parties, it does not end the tolerated trespasser's actual occupation, nor her obligation to pay for that occupation. Therefore a tolerated trespasser has the right to exclusive possession and has sufficient interest to sustain an action in nuisance.

9.2.6 Who may be sued in nuisance?

The creator of the nuisance will be liable for it, whether or not he is in occupation of the land. Furthermore, a landlord may be sued in nuisance where he authorises the creation or maintenance of a nuisance. It is clear from *Goldfarb v. Williams & Co.* (a 1945 High Court decision of Overend J.) that this authorisation may be express or implied. In that case, liability was imposed on the lessors of premises let to an employees' social and athletic club when the club operated dances and other social activities so as to cause a nuisance to the plaintiff. The premises were constructed in a fashion which transmitted the noise "with exceptional clearness and loudness" to the floors above and below.

In *Mowan v. Wandsworth London Borough Council* (2000), the Court of Appeal refused to hold the defendant council liable in nuisance for disturbance suffered by the plaintiff at the hands of a Miss Abrahart, a fellow tenant. Miss Abrahart, who suffered from a mental disorder, had on occasion subjected the plaintiff to excessive noise and to floods, and on one occasion even threatened Mrs Mowan's life. Staughton J. reiterated the principle that mere awareness of a nuisance and subsequent inactivity is not sufficient to ground a claim in nuisance against a lessor. The Irish decision, *Vitalograph (Ireland) Ltd v. Ennis U.D.C.* (1997) illustrates the circumstances under which a lessor may be liable in nuisance for injury suffered by its tenants, which was caused by trespassers on land retained by the lessor. This case will be analysed in our consideration of abatement (see 9.2.8 below).

A landlord will also be liable (notwithstanding that he has not authorised the nuisance) if he let the premises with the nuisance on them or where he has covenanted to repair and a nuisance is caused by his failure to comply with the covenant.

An occupier may be sued in nuisance where he creates a nuisance himself or where his servants, agents or visitors have created a nuisance which he has authorised.

9.2.7 The required duration of the interference

In *Cunard v. Antifyre* (1933), it was stated that "private nuisances, at least in the vast majority of cases, are interferences for a substantial length of time by owners or occupiers of property with the use or enjoyment of neighbouring property." Binchy (Annual Review of Irish Law, 1988, p. 435) notes that "where an interference is of a fleeting nature, which is unlikely to recur, the courts are reluctant to stigmatise it as a nuisance." This does not mean, however, that the tort of nuisance cannot be committed where damage results from a single act, such as the escape of gas or other inflammable material (*Midwood v. Manchester Corporation* (1905) and *Flynn v. Ross* (High Court, 1974)). Professor Binchy goes on to cite the Supreme Court decision in *Hanrahan v. Merck Sharp & Dohme* (1988), where Henchy J. stated that, to amount to nuisance, the plaintiffs would have to show that their use and enjoyment of their farm had been interfered with "over a substantial period of time."

9.2.8 Abatement

The right of an injured party to abate the nuisance is vividly illustrated in decisions such as *Lemmon v. Webb* (1884). It is settled law that the encroachment of roots and branches onto the land of another constitutes an actionable nuisance. In *Lemmon v. Webb,* the injured party was deemed to be entitled to take action by cutting the roots as soon as they projected onto his property. Indeed, a landowner in this situation may elect to apply for a *quia timet* injunction in anticipation of the encroachment.

Whilst the right to abate can enable occupiers to take steps to prevent the continuance of a nuisance, *Vitalograph (Ireland) Ltd v. Ennis U.D.C.* (1997) is an important recent decision which illustrates the circumstances where there may be a *duty* on an occupier to abate nuisances created on its property. Kelly J. (in the High Court) granted an interlocutory injunction in favour of the applicant, a company carrying on business on an industrial estate, requiring the defendants to restrain acts of nuisance committed by members of the travelling community on land adjacent to the entrance of the industrial estate, which was occupied by the defendants. Kelly J. noted that:

> Whilst [the County Council] has never given its permission for either the trespass or the tortious activities which are going on on its lands, neither has it done anything to bring them to an end in an effective

way. In my view, the County Council has with knowledge left the nuisance occurring on its lands.

In *Lynch v. Hetherton* (1990), the plaintiff's car was damaged in a collision with an ash tree which fell from the defendant's land onto the roadway. O'Hanlon J. found that the landowner was not liable in nuisance (or indeed negligence). He noted that:

> a land owner having on his lands a tree or trees adjoining a highway or his neighbour's lands is bound to take such care as a reasonable and prudent land owner would take to guard against the danger of damage caused by a falling tree.

In the instant case there was evidence that the tree in question, although rotten inside, seemed healthy from the outside. The trial judge was satisfied that there was no further duty on the defendant to employ an expert to assess the state of the trees.

9.3 Public nuisance

A public nuisance is both a crime and a tort. Its scope is somewhat difficult to define with exactitude, since it "covers a multitude of sins, great and small" (*Southport Corporation v. ESSO* (1954), Court of Appeal, *per* Denning L.J.). Public nuisance essentially consists of the injury to the reasonable comfort and convenience of the public or a section of the public. It was clearly stated in a Canadian decision (*Attorney General for Ontario v. Orange Productions* (1971)) that it is not necessary to establish that every member of the public, as distinct from a representative cross-section, has been affected.

Where the public, or some section of it, is injured by the public nuisance, only the Attorney General may take civil proceedings. McMahon & Binchy (2000, p.677) note that the reason for this limitation appears to be to prevent the taking of a multiplicity of actions, and to protect the wrongdoer against the risk of being punished a hundred times for the same cause. However, if the plaintiff as an individual member of the public has suffered particular damage over and above that suffered by the general public, then he will have the *locus standi* to maintain an action for public nuisance. In *Rose v. Miles* (1815), the defendant wrongfully obstructed a public canal, forcing the plaintiff to transport his goods across land. The Court held that due to the special damage suffered by the plaintiff, he could maintain an action in public nuisance. In *Boyd v. Great Northern Railway* (1895), the plaintiff, a doctor, who was delayed for 20 minutes at a level crossing by reason of the default of the defendant's servants, recovered 10 shillings' damages. The Court noted that the plaintiff had a "very large practice" and his time "was of pecuniary value."

In *Shoreham by Sea UDC v. Dolphin Canadian Proteins* (1972), the owner of a chicken by-product factory was held liable for the public nuisance created by the emission of nauseous smells. Donaldson J. considered the fact that the factory was long established in the area was a factor affecting the standards to be applied in judging whether or not there was a nuisance. He stated that the business had to be carried on in the manner causing the least practicable nuisance by applying standards which were reasonable when the nuisance was alleged to have been created. He found that the smell created a nuisance and concluded that it could be abated. Subject to minimal exceptions of human error and machinery breakdown, this abatement could be effected by improvements in covering and flooring of the factory, hooding and scrubbing equipment over all possible sources of smell, and better supervision of the state of raw materials and factory cleanliness and tidiness. The defendant undertook that it would not cause, after a period of nine months, any smells which would be a nuisance. In *Hassett v. O'Loughlin* (1943), O'Brien J. stated that nuisance on the highway can be anything that makes the highway unsafe or dangerous for the public to use.

In *Wandsworth London Borough Council v. Railtrack plc* (2001), the defendant was held liable for the public nuisance created by pigeons roosting under a railway bridge, which fouled the pavement below. On appeal, the Court of Appeal affirmed Gibbs J.'s decision and dismissed the defendant's appeal. It was stated that, in a case of a public nuisance, the liability of the landowner did not depend on whether the nuisance was created by his own or a third party's activities or by natural causes. The owner is liable if, having been aware of the existence of the nuisance and having the means and opportunity to abate it, he failed to do so.

Salmond (1992, pp. 58–59) pertinently states that private and public nuisances are not in reality two species of the same genus at all, for "there is no generic conception which includes the crime of making a bomb-hoax (*R v. Madden* (1975)) and the tort of allowing one's trees to overhang the land of a neighbour."

9.4 Defences to an action in nuisance

9.4.1 Legislative authority

Legislation may expressly or impliedly authorise the commission of what would otherwise be a nuisance at common law, *e.g.* the Air Navigation and Transport Act 1936. Statutory authorisation is an absolute defence, so that if a statute authorises the commission of a nuisance or if the nuisance is the inevitable consequence of the conduct permitted by the Act, then the statute acts as a complete defence to an action in nuisance. However, the authority will be lost if the conduct goes beyond the limits permitted by the statute. In *Kelly v. Dublin County Council* (1986), the defendant county council had carried on extensive road works in south Dublin pursuant to the Local Government Act 1925. This Act permitted the council to cause a nuisance in the discharge of their functions. The defendants established a busy storage depot close to the plaintiff's home causing much noise pollution in the area. O'Hanlon J. (in the High Court) held that the statutory authorisation to commit a nuisance was related to the maintenance and construction of roads. By setting up a storage depot, the defendant had engaged in an ancillary activity which was not protected by statute.

9.4.2 Prescription

Prescription is the acquisition of rights by virtue of long use. Prescription affords no defence for public nuisance. In an action for private nuisance, if the defendant can show 20 years' use as of right (*nec vi, nec clam, nec precario*, without force, secrecy or permission), then he may have acquired a right (in the form of an easement) to do what would otherwise be a nuisance. However, to establish this defence, the right in question must be capable of existing as an easement (*Re Ellenborough Park* (1955)).

In *Sturges v. Bridgman* (1879), the defendant had caused noise and vibration in the operation of his confectionery business for over 20 years. However, no complaints had been received about his activities in all that time. Then, in 1873, his neighbour, a physician, built consulting rooms adjacent to the site of the noisy operations. The defendant claimed to have acquired a prescriptive right to create the nuisance. The Court disagreed because the activity in question had not been a nuisance until the plaintiff had constructed his new consulting rooms.

9.4.3 Consent

If the plaintiff is held to have consented to the impugned acts, then his action in nuisance will fail. In *Thomas v. Lewis* (1937), the defendant opened a quarry and granted grazing rights to the plaintiff. The plaintiff then brought an action in nuisance alleging that the quarrying was interfering with his reasonable enjoyment of the land. The Court held that the plaintiff had impliedly consented to the impugned acts and this constituted a defence to an action based on the tort of nuisance.

9.4.4 Inevitable accident

In *Southport Corporation v. Esso Petroleum* (1954), the master of a ship took the decision to jettison 400 tons of oil in order to save the ship and his crew. The ship had developed a steering fault, and it was established at trial that his actions were appropriate in the circumstances. The oil was deposited on the plaintiff's foreshore, causing damage. Denning L.J. in the Court of Appeal held the discharge of oil was not a private nuisance since it did not involve the defendant's use of any land. However, he went on to hold that it was a public nuisance for which the defendant was liable to the plaintiff since the oil was discharged in such circumstances that it was likely to be carried on to the shore to the prejudice and discomfort of Her Majesty's subjects. The defendant had failed to show that the discharge of oil was an inevitable accident, *i.e.* a necessity which arose utterly without its fault. The defence of inevitable accident, which owes its origin to nineteenth-century shipping cases (such as *The Merchant Prince* (1892)), has been successfully invoked in negligence actions such as *Waugh v. Allan* (1964), where it defeated the claim of the plaintiff injured in an accident that was a consequence of the defendant driver's heart attack.

Further reading

McMahon & Binchy, *Law of Torts* (Butterworths, 2000), pp. 675–716; Quill, *Torts in Ireland* (Gill & Macmillan, 1999), pp. 190–216; Fleming, *The Law of Torts* (LBC, 1998), pp. 457–498; Weir, *A Casebook on Tort* (Sweet & Maxwell, 2000), pp. 425–452.

10. THE RULE IN *RYLANDS v. FLETCHER*

10.1 Introduction

A fault principle runs through tort law, making the imposition of strict liability exceptional. The application of the rule in *Rylands v. Fletcher* (1866–68) is one important instance where liability is imposed on a no-fault basis. The rule, which was developed by analogy with nuisance and case law on the liability of those who keep wild animals on their land, provides that a person who:

> ... for his own purposes brings on his lands and collects and keeps there anything likely to do mischief if it escapes, must keep it in at his peril, and, if he does not do so, is *prima facie* answerable for all the damage which is the natural consequence of its escape.

The rule continues to be one of the cornerstones of tort liability, despite sustained judicial and academic criticism. Judicial disapproval of the rule was manifested in a recent decision of the Australian High Court (*Burnie Port Authority v. General Jones Property* (1994)), which has had the effect of abolishing the rule for the escape of dangerous things in that jurisdiction.

10.2 *Rylands v. Fletcher*

The defendant in *Rylands v. Fletcher* operated the Ainsworth Mill in Lancashire, and the plaintiff owned the Red House Colliery nearby. In 1860, the defendant engaged independent contractors to construct a reservoir for the mill on land belonging to Lord Wilton. During the construction, a number of old mine shafts were discovered, but it was not realised that these indirectly connected with the plaintiff's colliery. The contractors were negligent in not ensuring that the filled-in shafts could bear the weight of water, and on December 11, 1860 the partially filled reservoir burst through to the plaintiff's colliery. An arbitrator established that the defendant was not guilty of negligence. Furthermore, no trespass had been committed since the damage caused by the flooding was not the direct consequence of the defendant's activity. Similarly, there was no liability in nuisance because the harm suffered by the plaintiff had been caused by a single escape. Nevertheless, the defendant was held liable. Blackburn J.'s decision in the Court of

Exchequer Chamber was affirmed with only slight modification by Lord Cairns in the House of Lords. The defendant was held liable because he had deliberately created a dangerous situation over which he had subsequently lost control.

It has been suggested that this epoch-making judgment owes much of its success to the broad scope of the principle announced and the strength of conviction of its creator and that a contrary decision would have had serious repercussions for the mining industry, which at that time was more important to the English economy than the surface-based milling industry. In support of this proposition, one may consider the hostile reception which *Rylands v. Fletcher* received on the eastern seaboard of the United States, where the milling industry was clearly more important than mining.

10.3 The scope of the rule

In his initial formulation of the rule, Blackburn J. imposed liability in respect of the escape of that which was "likely to do mischief if it escaped." Lord Cairns, on the other hand, appeared to modify the ambit of the rule by restricting the imposition of strict liability in these circumstances to the "non-natural use" of land. Clearly, Lord Cairns's conception of liability in this context is more restrictive and has justified the further limitation of the doctrine in subsequent decisions (*Miller v. Addie* (1934)). Kinder (1990, p. 318) notes that the original point of Lord Cairns's modification may have been simply to exclude liability for natural lakes. However, when Henchy J. considered the rule in *Hanrahan v. Merck Sharp & Dohme* in the Supreme Court (1988), he did not aver to the modification proposed by Lord Cairns, but instead defined the rule by reference to the escape of "a thing which is likely to do damage if it escaped."

The concept of non-natural use has been restrictively interpreted by the courts. In *Rickards v. Lothian* (1913), a decision of the Privy Council, Lord Moulton (at p. 280) stated that non-natural use "must be some special use bringing with it increased danger to others and must not merely be the ordinary use of the land or such a use as is proper for the general benefit of the community." Consequently, it was held that the accumulation of water for domestic supply does not come within the scope of the rule since it is a necessary feature of sanitary living. Similarly, in *Peters v Prince of Wales Theatre* (1943), the provision of water for use in garden sprinklers was deemed to be a natural use of land. In *Read v. Lyons* (1946), Lord Porter stated that "all the circumstances of time and practice of mankind must be taken into consideration so that what may be regarded as dangerous or non-natural may vary according to the circumstances." In the recent decision, *Stockport Metropolitan Borough Council v. British Gas Plc* (2001), the Court of Appeal refused to apply the rule where the plaintiff suffered damage caused by the escape of water from a three-inch service pipe under the defendant's control. Schiemann L.J. stated that no liability should attach to a defendant who lawfully uses his land for any purpose for which it might in the ordinary course of the enjoyment of the land be used. In this case, an embankment collapsed, having become saturated by water which had escaped from the aforementioned pipe. The collapse of the embankment exposed a now unsupported gas main and necessitated the unsuccessful plaintiff taking remedial action (at a cost of STG£94,000) in order to restore the support.

In the much-criticised decision of *Musgrove v. Pandelis* (1919), the Court of Appeal held that the keeping of a motor car in a garage with petrol in its tank was a non-natural use of land. This decision has not been followed, which is understandable given the proliferation of motor vehicles in modern society. In *A.G. v. Corke* (1933), the defendant allowed caravan dwellers to use his disused brickfield as a halting site. He was subsequently held liable under the rule when some of the caravan dwellers defecated on neighbouring land.

In *Healy v. Bray Urban District Council* (1961), the Supreme Court held that the defendant was not liable under the rule where the plaintiff's injury was caused by a rock which the defendant had not brought on to its land and which rolled down a hill onto other lands. The rock was "there as a result of natural forces operating in geological time ... They are, in short, the land itself and not things brought onto it" (*per* Kingsmill Moore J. at p. 15).

Professor Binchy (in a lecture delivered at Trinity College Dublin's Law School, *Torts 2000* Conference) has noted that the definition of non-natural use:

> ... pulls in opposing directions ... One can easily envisage a high risk process with a high social benefit (for example, the creation of an ammunition arsenal for the Defence Forces) and a low risk phenomenon with no significant social benefit (for example, a film star's swimming pool close to his neighbour's lands). For the court to make a decisive characterisation on the issue of unnatural user with the consequence of imposing strict liability for an escape may seem a blunt and somewhat arbitrary requirement. The law of negligence is far

more capable of making a nuanced assessment of such competing factors.

10.4 The boundaries of the rule

There exists a substantial degree of uncertainty concerning the historical basis for the development of the rule in *Rylands v. Fletcher.* Its birth was clearly influenced by other spheres of tortious liability, such as nuisance, and the special rules developed to govern liability for damage caused by animals. The rule itself was established before the emergence of modern negligence principles, and the absence of any other form of relief for the plaintiff in *Rylands* was probably a key influence in the creation of this extremely broad basis for imposing liability.

Evidence of an inter-relationship between the rule in *Rylands* and the tort of nuisance is strong. For example, an analogy has been drawn between the requirement of non-natural user under *Rylands* and that of unreasonableness in nuisance. Fleming (1998, p.466) disagrees with the legitimacy of this analogy, noting that "the reasonable user test ... bears no similarity to 'natural user' under *Rylands v. Fletcher*, notwithstanding the tentative suggestion by Lord Goff in *Cambridge Water* ..."

Winfield & Jolowicz (2002, pp. 550–551) note that while the rule had its origins in nuisance for most of this century, it had been regarded by the majority of lawyers as having developed into a distinct principle. This recognition of the rule as a truly independent tort may no longer be sustainable in light of the House of Lords' decision in *Cambridge Water Co. v. Eastern Counties Leather plc* (1994).

In an article entitled "The Boundaries of Nuisance" ((1949) 65 L.Q.R. 480), Professor Newark put forward his influential thesis that the rule's true significance was limited to the way in which it applied a general rule of strict liability in nuisance to situations where there was a claim for damages for an isolated escape, rather than the more usual ongoing state of affairs. This view was subsequently endorsed by the House of Lords in *Cambridge Water.* Professor Newark notes (at pp. 487–488) that *Rylands v. Fletcher*:

> ... is generally regarded as an important landmark, indeed a turning point – in the law of tort; but an examination of the judgments shows that those who decided it were quite unconscious of any revolutionary or reactionary principles implicit in the decision. They thought of it as calling for no more than a restatement of settled principles, and Lord Cairns went so far as to describe those principles as "extremely simple". And in fact the main principle involved was extremely sim-

ple, being no more than the principle that negligence is not an element in the tort of nuisance. It is true that Blackburn J in his great judgment in the Exchequer Chamber never once used the word "nuisance", but three times he cited the case of fumes escaping from an alkali works – a clear case of nuisance – as an instance of liability, under the rule which he was laying down. Equally it is true that in 1866 there were a number of cases in the reports suggesting that persons who controlled dangerous things were under a strict duty to take care, but as none of these cases had anything to do with nuisance Blackburn J. did not refer to them. But the profession as a whole, whose conceptions of the boundaries of nuisance were now becoming fogged, failed to see in *Rylands v. Fletcher* a simple case of nuisance. They regarded it as an exceptional case – and the rule in *Rylands v. Fletcher* as a generalisation of exceptional cases, where liability was to be strict on account of 'the magnitude of danger, coupled with the difficulty of proving negligence' [Pollock on Torts (14th edn, 1939), p 386] rather than on account of the nature of the plaintiff's interest which was invaded.

In *Cambridge Water*, Lord Goff determined that in light of the close relationship between the rule in *Rylands v. Fletcher* and the tort of nuisance, foreseeability of the occurrence of damage of the relevant type was a prerequisite for liability in both.

In *Cambridge Water*, the defendant had for some years used P.C.E. (an organochlorine) in its tanning trade. Continual small spillages had gradually built up a pool of the liquid under the land and contaminated the aquifer from which the plaintiffs drew their supply of water, forcing them to find another source, at a cost of nearly £1 million. P.C.E. evaporates quickly but is not readily water-soluble. When the contamination was taking place, it was not foreseeable to a skilled person that quantities of the chemical would accumulate in the aquifer; nor, even if this could have been foreseen, was it foreseeable that there would be any significant danger to the plaintiff's water. At the first instance, the trial judge held for the defendants on the basis that since the escape occurred in "an industrious setting," there was therefore no non-natural user. A unanimous House of Lords held that the defendant was not liable in damages for the contamination but on wholly different grounds. Their Lordships expressly disapproved of the trial judge's reasoning, but went on to hold that the rule was inapplicable unless it could be foreseen that damage of the relevant type would occur as the result of an escape.

The inter-relationship between the rule and the tort of negligence has also proved elusive. McMahon & Binchy (2000, pp.719–720) comment that under the rule in *Rylands:*

> ... the defendant is liable because he engaged in conduct which he knew or ought to have known was unduly risky. But what is this if it is not *negligence*? Surely, it may be said, the essence of negligence is taking an improper risk, whether the risk may result in immediate danger or damage at some unknown time in the future?

The *Cambridge Water* case clearly brought the rule closer to the tort of negligence by imposing a requirement that the damage caused by the escape be reasonably foreseeable, even though the escape itself need not have been. The decision of the Australian High Court in *Burnie Port Authority v. General Jones Property* (1994) effected an absorption of *Rylands v. Fletcher* into the tort of negligence in that jurisdiction, and has given rise to a general principle of non-delegable duties for hazardous activities. Whilst the scope of this new general principle is ill-defined, for present purposes it will suffice to state that a person who engages in a hazardous activity cannot escape liability for the harm which ensues merely by engaging an independent contractor to carry out the work.

The historical justification for the *Burnie* decision stems from the *dictum* of Lord Porter in *Read v. Lyons* (1946), where his Lordship suggested that it might become necessary at some future point to lay down principles for determining the concepts of "danger" and "non-natural use" for the purposes of the rule in *Rylands v. Fletcher*. In *Burnie,* it was noted that no such principles had been established in the intervening 47 years. According to the Australian High Court (Mason C.J.; Deane, Dawson, Toohey and Gaudron JJ. concurring):

> ... there is quite unacceptable uncertainty about the circumstances to give rise to its so called strict liability. The result is that the practical application of the rule in a case involving damage caused by the escape of a substance is likely to degenerate into an essentially unprincipled and ad hoc subjective determination of whether the particular facts of the case fall within undefined notions of what is special or not ordinary.

In *Burnie*, the plaintiff had a large quantity of frozen vegetables stored in cold rooms in a building which it partly occupied. The remainder of the building was occupied by the defendant, Burnie Port Authority, which also owned the building. Independent contractors engaged by Burnie Port Authority negligently caused a fire in the portion of the building occupied by the defendant. However, the fire spread and destroyed the plaintiff's goods. The Supreme Court of Tasmania had imposed liability on the defendant on the basis of the rule in *Rylands v. Fletcher*. On appeal, the question of what constitutes a non-natural use and the related difficulty in identifying dangerous items for the purposes of the principle led the Australian High Court to deal the rule a mortal blow. It substituted the old rule that one is strictly liable for the escape of that which he has accumulated on land, with a rule that such a person is under a "non-delegable" duty of care in respect of the activity involved in the accumulation.

It remains to be seen whether the *Burnie* decision will recommend itself to the Irish courts. In *McDonnell v. Ireland* (1997), Keane J. intimated adherence to more conventional notions of strict liability under the orthodox rule in *Rylands*, albeit in an *obiter* context. It does seem likely that the more restricted basis for establishing liability introduced by *Cambridge Water* will be followed in Ireland. Laffoy J. cited the decision in *Cambridge Water* with approval in *Superquinn v. Bray Urban District Council*, noting that:

> … [t]he nature of the liability of a defendant for the escape of dangerous things has been clarified recently by the House of Lords in *Cambridge Water Co v Eastern Counties Plc.* [1994] 2 AC 264, in which it was held that forseeablility of harm of the relevant type by the defendant is a prerequisite of the recovery of damages both in nuisance and under the rule in *Rylands v Fletcher*.

10.5 Escape

It is an essential element of liability under the rule in *Rylands v. Fletcher* that there be an escape from the defendant's property. For example, in *Read v. Lyons* (1946), the plaintiff, who was employed as an inspector at the defendant's munitions factory in Bedfordshire, was injured by an explosion whilst working in the shell-filling shop. The House of Lords held that the defendant could not be held liable under the rule since there was no escape from the premises. According to Viscount Simon (at p.168), "'Escape,' for the purpose of applying the proposition in *Rylands v Fletcher,* means escape from a place where the defendant has occupation of or control over land to a place which is outside his occupation or control."

McMahon & Binchy (2000, p.724) note that:

> ... [t]he requirement of escape has been criticised. There is something curious about a law which entitles a person, ordered by Ministerial direction to work in a munitions factory, to bring an action based on strict liability in respect of an explosion which injures him as he is approaching the factory but denies him this right where the explosion occurs when he is actually in the factory, where the danger of injury would be that much greater.

This line of criticism was foreseen by Lord Porter, who justified the subtlety of the distinction in such cases on the basis that *Rylands* was an exception to the general rule of fault-based liability and hence should be restricted.

10.6 Who can be sued under the rule?

It is clear that an occupier can be sued under the rule in *Rylands v. Fletcher* (*Benning v. Wong* (1969)), as can those persons who are on the land pursuant to a statutory authority or private permission. It is unclear whether an owner of land who is not in occupation of it can be sued under the rule where he authorised the accumulation. In *Smith v. Scott* (1972), it was decided that the rule could not be applied against a landlord who let his property to undesirable tenants, for a landlord who parted with possession of the demised property in favour of his tenant could not be regarded as controlling the property for the purposes of the tort.

10.7 Who can sue under the rule?

It is accepted that the entitlement to sue under the rule is not confined to adjoining occupiers and is bestowed upon any person who suffers damage as a consequence of the escape (*Healy v. Bray Urban District Council* (1961)). The restrictive approach taken by the House of Lords to the question of who may sue in nuisance (*Hunter v. Canary Wharf* (1997)) may well influence the adoption of a similarly restrictive attitude to who may sue under the rule in *Rylands v. Fletcher*. In *Hunter,* a mere licensee was precluded from maintaining an action in nuisance in respect of interference with his television signal caused by the erection of the defendant's skyscraper. It has been suggested (McMahon & Binchy, 2000, p.726) that under English law, non-adjoining occupiers may not be permitted to recover for personal (as opposed to material) injury under the rule. Decisions such as *Mullan v. Forrester* (1921) illustrate the Irish courts' greater willingness to permit recovery for all forms of injury, irrespective of whether or not the parties' properties are adjacent.

10.8 Defences

10.8.1 Consent of the plaintiff

If the plaintiff has either expressly or impliedly consented to the presence of the source of the danger, then the defendant is not liable under the rule. Fleming (1998, pp. 385–386) notes that "this principle has been most frequently invoked in cases where a lower tenant in a multiple dwelling suffers damage as the result of water seepage from an upper floor." Of course, in such situations, the defendant may avoid liability not only on the basis that his neighbours impliedly consented to the accumulation, but also because the accumulation itself was a natural use of the land (*Rickards v. Lothian* (1913).

10.8.2 Act of God

The existence of this defence was noted by Blackburn J. in *Rylands v. Fletcher*. He stated that a defendant could "excuse himself by showing that the escape was the consequence of ... an Act of God." The defence has been successfully relied upon in only one reported case, *Nichols v. Marsland* (1876). The courts have traditionally leaned against allowing this defence and thus, "gales in this country, heavy rainfalls in Wales and Scotland and heavy snowfalls in England have been held on the evidence, not to have been Acts of God" (McMahon & Binchy, 2000, p.730).

Recent consideration of the defence of Act of God took place in *Superquinn Ltd v. Bray U.D.C.* (1998). The plaintiff claimed damages under the rule in *Rylands v. Fletcher* for loss caused by flooding in the wake of "Hurricane Charlie". The fourth named defendant, Coillte Teoranta, was joined in the proceedings on the basis that it had created an artificial dam on the river Dargle that had contributed to the flooding, which in turn had damaged the plaintiff's property. The fourth named defendant attempted to rely on the defence of Act of God. Laffoy J. noted that "in order for the defence to succeed, it must be proved by the defendant that it was impossible to anticipate the occurrence or to guard effectively against it." On this basis, the defendant's defence failed, since it was found that the escape of the flood water could have been reasonably foreseen.

10.8.3 The default or sensitivity of the plaintiff

This defence absolves a party from liability where the plaintiff has unnecessarily exposed himself to the consequences of the escape from the defendant's property. In *Postmaster General v. Liverpool Corporation* (1923), the plaintiff negligently laid telegraph lines close to the defendant's electrical cables. The Court held that the plaintiff's default provided the defendant with a defence to an action framed under the rule.

The defence also exonerates defendants in circumstances where the damage suffered by the plaintiff is due to the latter's special sensitivity. For example, in *Eastern and South African Telegraph Co v. Cape Town Tramways* (1902), the Privy Council held that the rule in *Rylands v. Fletcher* did not apply to the facts, because the disturbances to the plaintiff's telegraph cable caused by the escape of electricity from the defendant's tramway system were the result of the plaintiff's special use of their property.

10.8.4 Act of a stranger

Winfield & Jolowicz (2002, p. 561) note that if the escape was caused by the independent act of a stranger which could not have been anticipated by the defendant, the rule in *Rylands v. Fletcher* will not be applicable. So, in *Box v. Jubb* (1879), the defendant escaped liability for damage caused when his reservoir overflowed partly because of the acts of a neighbouring reservoir owner. The defence does not extend to wrongful acts carried out by the defendant's employees or agents. Similarly, a defendant will be precluded from relying on the defence where the escape was caused by the act of a visitor to his premises.

10.8.5 Statutory authority

The defence of statutory authority is absolute in that no strict liability will attach to someone for an escape which occurs while they are carrying out a statutory duty. For the right to sue in nuisance in these circumstances, see *Kelly v. Dublin County Council* (1986).

Further reading

McMahon & Binchy, *Law of Torts* (Butterworths, 2000), pp. 717–734; Quill, *Torts in Ireland* (Gill & Macmillan, 1999), pp. 190–216; Fleming, *The Law of Torts* (LBC, 1998), pp. 375–390; Weir, *A Casebook on Tort* (Sweet & Maxwell, 2000), pp. 453–471; Kinder, *Casebook on Torts* (Blackstone Press, 1990), pp. 316–321; Jane Swanton, "Another Conquest in the Imperial Expansion of the Law of Negligence: Burnie Port Authority v General Jones Pty Ltd" (LEXIS) T.L.J. 1994 13.

11. OCCUPIERS' LIABILITY

11.1 Introduction

Irish law governing the tortious liability of occupiers for injury suffered by entrants whilst on their premises has been radically altered by the introduction of the Occupiers' Liability Act 1995. In the 20 years prior to its enactment, the common law was characterised by the courts' benevolent attitude to persons who entered land without permission and subsequently suffered injury. This benevolence was a consequence of the Supreme Court's decision in *McNamara v. Electricity Supply Board* (1975) where it was decided that a trespasser, in this case an infant who suffered serious injury while trespassing onto one of the defendant's sub-stations, was owed a common duty of care whilst on the occupier's land. As a result, an occupier was deemed liable if he failed to take "reasonable care" for the trespasser's safety whilst on his land. The *McNamara* decision constituted a sharp break with the common law as it existed prior to 1975 whereby an occupier would only be liable for injury suffered by a trespasser whilst on the occupier's land if the occupier intentionally caused the injury or acted with reckless disregard for the trespasser's safety (*Addie & Sons v. Dumbreck* (1929)). This restriction on the duty owed by occupiers towards trespassers was clearly part of the legacy of the dominance of the propertied classes which prevailed at that time and "represented the one piece of dry land which was not swamped when Lord Atkin, in *Donoghue v Stevenson,* opened the floodgates of the modern law of negligence" (McMahon & Binchy, 2000, p.299).

Four distinct categories of entrant were recognised prior to the enactment of the 1995 Act, the contractual entrant, the invitee, the licensee and the trespasser. The contractual entrant was someone who was contractually entitled to visit the premises in question, *e.g.* a paying race-goer at a race meeting. The invitee was someone who was invited on to the premises for the purpose of conferring a material advantage on the occupier, such as a customer entering a shop or a tourist viewing an attraction (*Thomas v. Leitrim County Council* (1998)). The licensee was someone who entered the premises on foot of a license, his entry being either permitted or at least tolerated. The trespasser was defined as someone who enters land without license, invitation or contractual right.

Prior to *McNamara,* the common duty of care *simpliciter* was only extended to contractual entrants. The invitee's presence on his property obliged the occupier to take reasonable care to prevent damage from unusual danger of which the occupier knew or ought to have known. For example, in *Doyle v. Magill* (1999), a decision of McCracken J. based on facts which occurred prior to the coming into force of the 1995 Act, the defendant was the occupier of a three-storey over-basement dwelling whose employee had invited the plaintiff and his wife to a New Year's party. On leaving the defendant's premises after the party, the plaintiff had walked onto the defendant's rose-bed in attempting to access the driver's door of his car, from where he fell into a sunken area at the front of the house created to permit light to permeate the basement. It was held that the occupier was not liable for injuries sustained by the plaintiff. The trial judge held that this sunken basement area did not constitute an unusual danger because the premises in question was "a very old large house of the type which is not uncommon in rural Ireland, and a feature of which is a basement and basement area of this nature". McCracken J. stated that "the class of persons to whom the plaintiff belongs (invitees) ought to have known this, and in my view the existence of an area of this nature is not an unusual danger to such a class of persons."

An even lower standard of care was owed to licensees. The occupier's duty was limited to warning the licensee of dangers of which he was *actually* aware. Finally, and as previously discussed, the only duty owed by an occupier to a trespasser prior to the Supreme Court's decision in *McNamara* was to avoid intentionally harming the trespasser or acting with reckless disregard for his safety.

While the four categories survived the *McNamara* decision, it nonetheless "blurred these distinctions and shows the adoption of a reasonable care standard in the context of occupiers' liability" (Doherty, *Annotation to the Act,* I.C.L.S.A., 1995). The farming community were particularly unhappy about the state of the law post *McNamara.* According to Professor McMahon (in an article in the *Law Society Gazette,* December 1995), "they feared that recreational users on their land and without their knowledge might sue in respect of injuries suffered as a result of dangers on the land." Farmers' fears were probably exaggerated in light of the difficulties encountered by plaintiff trespassers in establishing the requisite degrees of proximity and reasonable foreseeablity. The law on occupiers' liability has been subjected to various forms of scrutiny and proposals for reform. The Law Reform Commission published a review (*Consultation Paper on Occupiers'*

Liability, 1993) and report (*Report on Occupiers' Liability,* 1994) on the liability of occupiers.

11.2 The 1995 Act

The Occupiers' Liability Act 1995 effected a radical reform of the law and represents the implementation of the majority of the Law Reform Commission's proposals. Under the Act, visitors are present by permission, agreement or by right and the occupier owes a common duty of care to them. This duty is defined in the Act as a duty "to take such care as is reasonable in all the circumstances ... to ensure that a visitor to the premises does not suffer injury or damage by reason of any danger existing thereon" (section 3). The duty owed to an entrant is contingent upon the category within which he falls.

11.2.1 The categories of entrant

This common duty of care which is owed to visitors equates with the duty of care in negligence and may be affected by the plaintiff's contributory negligence or where the visitor was in the company of another who would be expected to have supervised the visitor.

Trespassers survive as an identifiable group, but under the Act the standard of care owed to them is substantially lower than that provided by *McNamara*. In place of the plaintiff-friendly common duty to take reasonable care, the older common law standard to be found in earlier cases such as *Indermaur v. Dames* (1866) and *Addie & Sons v. Dumbreck* (1929) is applied. The occupier owes a duty to trespassers (and recreational users) to avoid injuring them intentionally and to avoid acting with reckless disregard for their safety (section 4). It may be noted that this represents a lower standard than that of gross negligence proposed by the Law Reform Commission in its Consultation Paper in 1993.

The term "occupier" is defined in relation to the premises as meaning:

> ... a person exercising such *control* over the state of the premises that it is *reasonable* to impose upon that person a duty towards an entrant in respect of a particular danger thereon and, where there is more than one occupier of the same premises, the extent of the duty of each occupier towards an entrant depends on the degree of control each of them has over the state of the premises and the particular danger thereon and whether, as respects each of them, the entrant concerned

is a visitor, recreational user or trespasser (section 1) (parentheses added).

"Entrant" is defined in relation to a danger existing on premises as "a person who enters on the premises and is not the sole occupier" (section 1).

"Premises" are defined as *including* "land, water and any fixed or moveable structures thereon and also includes vessels, vehicles, trains, aircraft and other means of transport." Gardens (*Burr v. Eyre* (1998)), lifts (*Haseldine v. Daw* (1941)), and even digging machines (*Bunker v. Charles Brand & Son Ltd* (1969)) have been deemed to come within the definition of premises. In *Weldon v. Mooney & Campbell (trading as Fingal Coaches)* (2001), a decision of O'Caoimh J. in the High Court, it was implicitly accepted that the plaintiff's chosen method of conveyance, the luggage compartment of the defendant's bus, came within the meaning of the term "premises". In the context of premises, "danger" is defined (at section 1) as meaning "a danger due to the state of the premises"; therefore liability for injury caused by an activity carried out on the occupier's premises is determined by utilising common law negligence principles.

11.2.2 Recreational users

The 1995 Act, in response to the farming lobby's concerns, created a new category of entrant, the recreational user. The effect of the creation of this category of entrant was to diminish the duty of care owed to those who, whilst not on the land pursuant to the granting of the occupier's permission, nonetheless were tolerated (and were therefore not to be considered trespassers) by those who had the right to exclude them.

A "recreational user" is defined in the Act as an entrant who is present with or without permission or implied invitation free of charge (other than a reasonable charge in respect of the cost of providing vehicle-parking facilities), including entrants to national monuments under the National Monuments Act 1930, for the purpose of engaging in a recreational activity. Excluded from this definition, however, are members of the occupier's own family who are ordinarily resident on the premises and also entrants who are expressly invited onto the premises for social reasons by the occupier or a member of his family. Such lawful entrants are deemed to achieve the more elevated status of "visitor". Section 1 defines "recreational activity" as "any such activity conducted in the open air including any sporting activity, scientific research and nature study so conducted, exploring caves, visiting sites and buildings of historical, architectural, traditional, artistic, archaeological or scientific importance".

11.2.3 Recklessness defined

In determining whether the occupier's conduct was reckless, all the circumstances will be taken into account. Section 4(2) of the Act specifically refers to the following circumstances:

(a) whether the occupier knew or should have known of the danger on the premises;

(b) whether the occupier knew or should have known of the likelihood of the persons' presence on the premises or their likely presence in the vicinity of the danger on the premises;

(c) whether the danger was one which the occupier might reasonably be expected to provide protection for the entrant;

(d) the burden on the occupier of eliminating the danger, taking into account the difficulty, the expense or the impracticality of removing the danger;

(e) the nature of any warnings given by the occupier;

(f) the conduct which the entrant may be expected to take for his own safety.

Pursuant to section 4(2)(h), "in determining whether or not an occupier has acted with reckless disregard regard shall be had to all the circumstances of the case including, the nature of any warning given by the occupier or another person of the danger." This provision confers significance on all forms of warning issued by the occupier to those trespassing on his lands or those using it for recreational purposes. Of course, the more objectively appropriate the warning given, the less likely that the occupier will be deemed to have been reckless in connection with the injury suffered by the plaintiff.

In *Weldon v. Mooney & Campbell*, the plaintiff suffered serious injury having boarded and subsequently fallen from the luggage compartment of the defendant's bus whilst in transit. O'Caoimh J. stated that the plaintiff's cause of action (based on the defendant's employee's alleged knowledge that the plaintiff was being carried in the luggage compartment) could be framed under common law negligence principles irrespective of whether:

... any case of acting with "reckless disregard" for the Plaintiff can be sustained [under the Occupiers' Liability Act, 1995] [I]f as alleged the Defendants knowingly permitted persons to use the luggage compartment and drove the bus in circumstances where it was known that the Plaintiff was in the luggage compartment, an issue of negligence remains.

This case highlights the fact that liability under the statutory scheme runs in parallel with and in no way excludes the application of common law negligence principles.

Section 4(3) provides that an occupier's statutory duty towards trespassers does not extend to someone who either enters his premises for the purpose of committing an offence or, where present on the premises, commits an offence. Such a person may only recover from the occupier when a court determines that recovery is "in the interest of justice". This jurisdiction is likely to be exercised in circumstances where the crime is not serious, in which case the more conventional recklessness standard will be applied by the court. McMahon & Binchy (2000, pp. 327–328) note that:

> It is not necessary that the person should have entered the premises where the injury occurs for the purposes of committing an offence there. A would-be thief who enters one premises as a means of access to another, where he intends to steal, falls within the section. Conversely, a person who goes into a café to pass the time before a bank robbery has not entered the café "for the purpose of" committing an offence, but merely with the intention of doing so afterwards, there being no connection between the café and the bank.

11.2.4 Modification of the occupier's duty

Section 5(1) provides that an occupier may by express agreement or notice extend his or her duty towards entrants. Conversely, pursuant to section 5(2)(a) an occupier may, either by express agreement or notice, restrict, modify or exclude his or her duty towards visitors. However, under section 5(2)(b) such a restriction, modification or exclusion will only be effective if it is reasonable in all the circumstances, and the occupier has taken steps to bring the notice to the attention of the visitor.

It is important to note that an occupier is prevented from lowering his "common duty of care" to visitors below that standard which is owed to trespassers and recreational users. Section 5(3) provides that:

[i]n respect of a danger existing on premises, a restriction, modification or exclusion referred to in subsection (2) shall not be taken as allowing an occupier to injure a visitor or damage the property of a visitor intentionally or to act with reckless disregard for a visitor or the property of a visitor.

11.2.5 Structures on premises

An occupier's duty to recreational users may also be extended in connection with a structure on the premises which is used or was intended for use primarily by recreational users. Pursuant to section 4(4) of the Act, "the occupier shall owe a duty towards such users in respect of such a structure to take reasonable care to maintain the structure in a safe condition." Examples of such structures would include dressing-rooms in public sports grounds, playground equipment and picnic tables in highway lay-bys. It is irrelevant that the occupier did not erect or install the structure. However, section 4(4) goes on to provide that:

… where a stile, gate, footbridge or other similar structure on premises is or has been provided not for use primarily by recreational users, the occupier's duty towards a recreational user thereof in respect of such structure shall not be extended by virtue of this subsection.

The Act, in creating a new category of entrant in the form of the recreational user, has created a subtle distinction between those who come onto land for the purpose of engaging in a recreational activity and those who are there to engage in a social activity. In considering the distinction between recreational users and social visitors, Quill (1999, p.141) comments that: "the distinction between [them] appears to be that social visitors are persons whose presence is desired by the occupier (or the occupier's family), whereas recreational users are those whose presence is tolerated."

The duty on the occupier may be *extended* by express agreement without the limitations imposed by section 5(2)(b).

Section 7 of the Act provides that the occupier of premises shall not be liable for injury or damage caused by a danger existing on the premises due to the negligence of an independent contractor, provided the occupier has taken all reasonable care in the selection of the independent contractor and ought not to have noticed that the work was not properly carried out. However, section 8(c) of the Act goes on to provide that:

nothing in this Act shall be construed as affecting any enactment or any rule of law relating to any liability imposed on an occupier for a tort committed by another person in circumstances where the duty imposed on the occupier is of such a nature that its performance may not be delegated to another person.

In this way, an occupier's non-delegable liability for "ultra hazardous" activities carried out on his land has been retained.

The Act provides for recovery for a wide range of injuries suffered by entrants. Under section 1(1), "damage" includes loss of property and injury to an animal. "Injury" includes loss of life, any disease and any impairment of physical or mental condition. Quill (1999, p.146) suggests that an entrant who suffers economic loss due to the state of the occupier's premises should be able to recover for such loss since recovery is not expressly excluded under the Act. This proposition has yet to be tested by the courts.

Further reading

McMahon & Binchy, *Law of Torts* (Butterworths, 2000), pp. 299–336; Quill, *Torts in Ireland* (Gill & Macmillian, 1999), pp. 137–146; Fleming, *The Law of Torts* (LBC, 1998), pp. 499–529; Law Reform Commission, *Report on Occupiers Liability* (Government Publications Office, 1994); Farrelly & Bundock, "Dangerous premises and liability to trespassers" (March 2, 2001) 151 New Law Journal 309.

12. TRESPASS TO LAND

12.1 Introduction

A person is guilty of trespass to land where, in the absence of lawful justification, he intentionally or negligently, enters or remains on or brings something into contact with land in the possession of another. The action is very closely related to nuisance in the sense that both torts seek to vindicate the property rights of the individual. However, a marked difference exists between these forms of action; trespass to land is concerned with direct interferences, whereas nuisance also encompasses indirect interferences with land.

As with all forms of trespass, the tort is actionable *per se*, thus "every invasion of property, be it ever so minute, is a trespass" (*Entick v. Carrington* (1765)). However, it may be noted that the "invasion of property" does not have to be to the detriment of the landowner. For example, in the *Case of Thorns* (1466), the defendant was found guilty of trespass where he had entered onto the plaintiff's property in order to retrieve some cuttings he had dropped there.

Nor is it necessary that the conduct giving rise to an action in trespass to land be intentional. For example, in *Basely v. Clarkson* (1681), the defendant was found guilty of trespass where he cut the grass on the plaintiff's land, mistakenly believing that that the land was his own property. However, in order to be actionable, the act of the defendant must be voluntary. Davitt P. posited the following example in *O'Brien v. McNamee* (1953):

> If a man is sitting on a wall and is pushed so that he falls into someone else's land and thereby commits a trespass, his act is involuntary and he is not liable in tort, but if he is shooting and thinks he has a right to be on the particular land, when in fact he has no such right, then he is liable for trespass even though he has no intention of trespassing.

12.2 Constitutional protection

The protection afforded by the tort of trespass to land is supplemented *vis-à-vis* dwellings by Article 40.5 of the Constitution, which provides that "[t]he dwelling of every citizen is inviolable and shall not be forci-

bly entered save in accordance with law." In *People (A.G.) v. O'Brien*
(1965), Walsh J. (in the Supreme Court) stated:

> … the reference to forcible entry is an intimation that forcible entry
> may be permitted by law but that in any event the dwelling of every
> citizen is inviolable save where entry is permitted by law and that, if
> necessary, such law may permit forcible entry.

12.3 Direct interference

One of the central elements of the tort of trespass on land is the existence of an unlawful direct interference with property in the possession
of another. Thus, in *Whelan v. Madigan* (1978), it was held that striking
a door with the intent of breaking it down amounted to a trespass, and
in *Westripp v. Baldock* (1938), it was held that a trespass was committed where the defendant placed a ladder against the plaintiff's wall
without his permission. The interference with the plaintiff's possession
of property need only be minimal. For example, in *Wilcox v. Kettel*
(1937), an intrusion of 50 centimetres by a concrete foundation was
held to be a trespass.

12.4 Abuse of right of entry

A person will become a trespasser where he enters on property with
permission ostensibly for one purpose, and uses such permission for
other purposes beyond the boundaries of the consent initially agreed.
This issue was raised in *DPP v. McMahon* (1987), which concerned the
admissibility of illegally obtained evidence. Plainclothes members of
the gardaí entered the defendant's premises in order to investigate
alleged breaches of the Gaming and Lotteries Act 1956. The gardaí did
not have a search warrant as required by the Act. The defendant argued
that the evidence which had been obtained upon entry was inadmissi-
ble. Justification for the entry of the gardaí was made on two grounds:
(i) they had implied permission to enter the premises as members of
the public; and (ii) they had a right of entry onto such premises under
the licensing laws. However, the Court held that the gardaí had abused
their right of entry and were trespassers. It was held that the implicit
permission bestowed on the public to enter the premises for the purposes of consuming alcohol did not extend to members of the gardaí
whose desire to enter the premises did not relate to such a purpose.
Further, the statutory authority to enter such premises under the licens-

ing Acts was limited to investigations of suspected breaches of the licensing laws and did not extend to investigations regarding the Gaming and Lotteries Act. The entry amounted to a trespass and the evidence obtained as a result was not admissable.

12.5 Trespass *ab initio*

A person who enters property with lawful permission may become a trespasser *ab initio* (from the moment of entry) where he exceeds such authority following entry. A person can only become a trespasser *ab initio* in such circumstances where he commits an act of positive misfeasance and cannot become a trespasser *ab initio* for mere nonfeasance. The historical origins of the principle can be traced back to *The Six Carpenters Case* (1610), where the defendants refused to pay for wine and bread they had consumed in an inn. It was held that while they had abused their right to enter, they were not trespassers *ab initio* (therefore had not committed an act of trespass), since their refusal to pay for the wine and bread amounted to nonfeasance. The principle was recently applied in *Webb v. Ireland* (1988), where the plaintiffs had lawfully entered property in order to view a national monument. They were deemed to be trespassers *ab initio*, however, once they dug up the earth in pursuit of treasure trove. Notwithstanding the lawful nature of their entry, the plaintiffs became trespassers from the moment of entry once they began their excavation.

12.6 Trespass over and under the land

He who owns the land is said to own the property right up to heaven and down to the middle of the earth. Thus, an action for trespass may lie where the defendant encroaches on the plaintiff's airspace, even where the defendant makes no contact with the land itself. In *Kelsen v. Imperial Tobacco Co.* (1957), the defendant attached an advertising sign to the side of its building, which was adjacent to the plaintiff's property. The sign protruded eight inches onto the plaintiff's airspace and the defendant was liable in trespass as a result. Similarly, in *Keating & Co. Ltd v. Jervis Shopping Centre Ltd* (1996) the operation of a crane encroaching on the plaintiff's airspace was held to be capable of constituting a trespass to the plaintiff's land. In *Bernstein v. Skyviews Ltd* (1978), the defendant took an aerial photograph of the plaintiff's house from an aeroplane. It was held that as the flight took place at a height which did not interfere with the defendant's enjoyment of his property, an action in trespass could not succeed. Griffiths J. noted that a strict application of the general maxim would lead to the "absurdity of a trespass being committed by a satellite every time it passes over a suburban garden." The common law position has been qualified under statute pursuant to section 55 of the Air Navigation and Transport Act 1936, as amended by section 47(1) of the Air Navigation and Transport Act 1988, which provides that no action in trespass or nuisance shall lie where the flight of any aircraft is at a height which is reasonable having regard to all the circumstances.

The owner of the subsoil of land may also bring an action where it has been unlawfully interfered with. Thus, boring a tunnel for mining purposes into property owned by another will be actionable in trespass (*Bulli Coal Mining Co. v. Osborne* (1899)). The right to bring such an action may be subject to statute (for example, pursuant to section 12 of the Minerals Development Act, 1979). The question of whether actions in trespass to the subsoil should be entertained where the trespass does not affect the plaintiff's enjoyment of the land arose in the American case of *Edwards v. Sims* (1929), where an entrance to a cave was situated on the defendant's land. The cave ran over 300 hundred feet beneath the plaintiff's land. The defendant opened the cave as a tourist attraction and commenced charging the public a fee to enter. The plaintiff successfully sued for trespass to his land and a share in the profits the defendant had earned. Prosser & Keeton have commented that this decision is "dog-in-the-manger law" since the caves could be of no use to the plaintiff without the defendant's actions as he had no access to them. However, the dissenting judgment of Logan J. in the case is noteworthy where he expresses the view that the general right of an owner to all above and below the land should be limited to so much of the land over which the plaintiff could exercise control, stating: "No man can bring up from the depth of the earth the Stygian darkness and make it serve his purposes, unless he has the entrance to it."

The principle in *Edwards* has been adopted subsequently in the American case of *Boehringer v. Montalto* (1931) where the court held that the laying of a sewer 150 feet below the plaintiff's property could not amount to an act of trespass.

12.7 Trespass on the highway

The public are entitled to use the highway in any reasonable manner. However, if they use the highway for unreasonable purposes, then they will be liable in trespass. In *Iveagh (Earl) v. Martin* (1961), Paull J. commented:

> On a highway I may stand still for a reasonably short time, but I must not put my bed upon the highway and permanently occupy a portion of it. I may stoop to tie up my shoelace, but I may not occupy a pitch and invite people to come upon it and have their hair cut. I may let my van stand still long enough to deliver and load goods but I must not turn my van into a permanent stall.

Where the highway is being used for an improper purpose, the owner of the subsoil (usually the owner of the adjacent property) may bring an action in trespass. Thus, in *Hickman v. Maisey* (1900), the defendant was a "racing tout" who walked up and down the highway adjoining the plaintiff's property, while viewing the form of the plaintiff's horses. The plaintiff as owner of the subsoil, was held to be entitled to bring an action in trespass against the defendant where he abused his right to use the highway.

12.8 Continuing trespass

If a trespass is ongoing, it will be deemed to be a continuing trespass and will give rise to actions *de die in diem* (as long at it lasts). In *Holmes v. Wilson* (1839), the defendants trespassed on the plaintiff's land when installing buttresses to support the construction of a road. The defendant was further held to be liable for a continuing trespass when, following the initial action, he failed to remove the offending buttresses.

A continuing trespass must be distinguished from a once-off action, such as cutting another's hedge or cutting down a tree on the property of another. Such contact will only give rise to a single action. In *Clarke v. Midland Great Western Railway Co.* (1895), the defendant disrupted the flow of a stream on the plaintiff's property in order to supply its station with water. The entry onto the property to disrupt the stream was a once off. However, it was held that as the defendant was receiving an ongoing benefit from the water, the disruption caused amounted to a continuing trespass. Holmes J. examined the distinction between a once-off trespass and a continuing one in his judgment, noting that:

> The element of continuity must, I think, be looked for not in the right interrupted but in the acts that cause the interruption. Where a man commits a trespass by placing something on another's land, it is reasonable to regard him as responsible for its continuance until he takes

away what is in its nature removeable, or until the owner of the lands by refusing him permission to remove it adopts what has been done. But a tree cut down is gone forever. Compensation can be made for it, but it cannot be brought back. So, too, in the case of an excavation; it may no doubt be filled up, but not so as to make the excavated place what it was before. An equivalent can be given, but restoration, strictly speaking, is impossible.

According to Quill (1999, p.167), the principle ensures that a trespasser cannot simply "purchase" a right to place something on the property of another. If only one action were allowed for trespasses of this nature, then the defendant could place an object on the property, pay damages for his trespass and continue to derive a benefit from having the object on the property.

12.9 Who can sue?

The tort seeks to protect a person's right to possession of property. Thus, a tenant in possession may bring an action (*Whelan v. Madigan* (1978)). Indeed, Quill (1999, p. 162) has pointed out that the person who sues for trespass need not be legally in possession of the property in question so long as he has a better right to possession than the trespasser.

It is not a good defence for a person to argue that the person in possession has no right to sue because that right properly rests with a third party. This principle is known as *jus tertii*. Salmond & Heuston (1992, p. 397) have stated:

> the mere de facto and wrongful possession of land is a valid title of right against all persons who cannot show a better title in themselves, and is therefore sufficient to support an action of trespass against such persons.

In *Petrie v. Owners of SS Rostrevor* (1898), the plaintiff used an area of foreshore as an oyster bed. The plaintiff, who did not possess legal title to the foreshore, brought an action in trespass. The court held that "Petrie, by placing the oysters on the foreshore ha[d] become possessed of it de facto, and [was] consequently in legal possession as against all the world except its true owner." However, the plaintiff's action was not ultimately successful, as the defendant had received permission of the true legal owners of the foreshore when removing their stricken ship.

12.10 Defences

12.10.1 Consent

The owner/occupier of property may give his consent to the defendant's entry. In such a situation, no action in trespass can lie unless the entrant abuses his right of entry (*DPP v. McMahon* (1987)). Consent to enter the property of another is given in the form of a licence and such permission may be express or implied. A bare licence is a right of entry granted notwithstanding the absence of consideration. Such a licence may be withdrawn at any time, but the entrant must be allowed a reasonable time to leave the property. A licence coupled with an interest is a licence supported by consideration (*Hurst v. Picture Theatres Ltd* (1915)). Such a licence can only be revoked according to the terms of the licence or agreement.

12.10.2 Actions of third parties

In order to succeed in an action for trespass to land, it must be shown that the trespass was committed either intentionally or negligently. Therefore, if a person enters the property of another unlawfully as a result of the conduct of a third party, an action will not lie. In *Moloney v. Stephens* (1945), the owner of cattle was held to be not liable in trespass where his cattle were chased onto the plaintiff's field by a third party.

12.10.3 Lawful justification

Where a person enters property with lawful justification, he will not be held liable under the tort of trespass to land, provided that he does not abuse his right of entry. The right of public officials to enter property under such circumstances is heavily regulated by statute law. For example, section 6 of the Criminal Law Act 1997 entitles gardaí to enter premises to arrest (with or without a search warrant) in certain circumstances. Further powers to search land and premises are bestowed on members of the gardaí pursuant to section 23 of the Misuse of Drugs Act 1977, as amended by section 12 of the Misuse of Drugs Act 1984.

12.10.4 Necessity

A person entering property without permission may have a defence to an action in trespass where it can be established that such entry was on foot of an emergency. However, it must be shown that the entry was reasonable in the circumstances. In *Cope v. Sharpe* (1912), a fire broke out on X's land. X's employees attempted to put the fire out. Z owned a neighbouring property, where pheasants were nesting. Z's gamekeeper, in an attempt to protect his employer's property, set another fire to act as a firewall. X's employees extinguished the fire on his land and Z was sued for trespass. It was held that Z was not liable, since his employee had acted reasonably in the circumstances and was motivated by a desire to protect his employer's property from a very real and imminent danger. The action of the defendant must be necessary and not negligent. In *Rigby v. Chief Constable of Northamptonshire* (1985), the plaintiff's action in trespass to land, where the defendant threw a can of CS gas into the plaintiff's premises in order to remove a dangerous criminal inside, was unsuccessful, as the defendant's actions were deemed to be necessary.

12.11 Remedies

12.11.1 Damages and injunction

A plaintiff is entitled to receive damages for all acts of trespass committed on his property. Where the trespass is of a trivial nature, the damages awarded are likely to be nominal. The court may also award an injunction in appropriate situations, *e.g.* where the trespass is continuing. In *Keating & Co. Ltd v. Jervis Shopping Centre Ltd* (1996), the defendant was undertaking extensive development work on buildings adjacent to the plaintiff's licensed premises. The plaintiff sought an injunction prohibiting the jib of a crane used by the defendant from entering the airspace above its property. Keane J., in refusing the plaintiff's interlocutory application for an injunction, held that the plaintiff had failed to establish that an award of damages at the trial of the action would be inadequate.

12.11.2 Re-entry

A person entitled to possession of the property may lawfully re-enter it, recover possession and forcibly remove the trespasser, provided he uses reasonable force (*Hemmings v. Stoke Poges Golf Club* (1920)).

12.11.3 Mesne profits

The plaintiff may bring an action against a trespasser for losses he may have suffered as a result of being dispossessed of the property. An action for mesne profits will entitle the plaintiff to sue the defendant for any profits the latter has made as a result of his wrongful occupation of the property and to recover damages for the deterioration of the property together with the costs associated with recovering the property (*Goodtitle v. Tombs* (1770)).

Further reading

McMahon & Binchy, *Law of Torts* (Butterworths, 2000), pp. 653–674; Quill, *Torts in Ireland* (Gill & Macmillian, 1999), pp. 147–189; Fleming, *The Law of Torts* (LBC, 1998), pp. 45–57; Rogers, *Winfield & Jolowicz on Tort* (Sweet & Maxwell, 2002), pp. 324–327.

13. TRESPASS TO THE PERSON

13.1 Introduction

The tort of trespass to the person affords protection to persons from unlawful invasions of their bodily integrity. Fawsitt J. outlined the safeguards provided by the tort in *Dullaghan v. Hillen* (1957), stating:

> Security for the person is among the first conditions of civilized life. The law, therefore, protects us, not only against actual hurt and violence, but against every kind of bodily interference and restraint not justified or excused by allowed cause, and against the present (immediate) apprehension of any of these things.

Trespass to the person is actionable *per se*. As proof of actual damage is not the gist of the action, the scope and effectiveness of the tort is greatly enhanced. Indeed, Lord Reid has in *S v. McC* (1972) advised against any dilution of this principle, noting that:

> We have too often seen freedom disappear in other countries not only by *coups d'etat* but by gradual erosion; and it is often the first step that counts. So it would be unwise to make even minor concessions.

Actions in trespass to the person share certain characteristics, the existence of which are necessary in order to ground an action. The impugned conduct must be voluntary. (*Scott v. Shepherd* (1773)) and must be carried out intentionally or in a negligent manner. The defendant will be liable where he intends the consequences arising from his act. He will also be liable where, although he did not desire the consequences of his act, they were nonetheless a foreseeable result of his intentional conduct. This distinction was considered in *Gibbon v. Pepper* (1695) as follows:

> [I]f I ride upon a horse, and [one party] whips the horse, so that he runs away with me and runs over any other person, he who whipped the horse is guilty of the battery, and not me. But if I by spurring was the cause of such accident, then I am guilty. In the same manner, if A takes the hand of B and with it strikes C, A is the trespasser and not B.

In an action for trespass to the person, the burden of proof rests on the plaintiff, who must establish that the defendant's conduct directly caused the interference complained of. Once that is established, the burden of proof shifts to the defendant, who must then establish that the conduct was neither intentional nor negligent (*O'Conghaile v. Wallace* (1938)).

The general tort of trespass to the person is subdivided into three distinct torts, namely battery, assault and false imprisonment.

13.2 Battery

A person commits a battery where he intentionally, and without the consent of the victim, applies direct force to that person (*Dullaghan v. Hillen* (1957)). Winfield & Jolowicz (1994, p.63) have defined the tort as "the intentional and direct application of force to another person".

As the tort is actionable *per se*, actual damage does not have to result. Thus, in *R. v. Cotesworth* (1704), the act of spitting at another was deemed to be a battery. Similarly, in *Humphries v. O'Connor* (1864), it was held that the action of a policeman removing a lily from the plaintiff's coat was a battery and in *White v. Store Security Ltd* (1985), the defendant's agent's act of grabbing hold of the plaintiff was deemed to be an actionable trespass.

Not every form of physical contact will constitute a battery. An early attempt to distinguish lawful from unlawful contact was made by Holt C.J. in *Cole v. Turner* (1704), when he said that, "the least touching of another in anger is a battery." However, the tort is not limited to aggressive actions. In the English case of *Collins v. Wilcock* (1984), it was suggested that touching would not amount to a battery where such contact was "generally acceptable in the ordinary conduct of general life." However, in *Wilson v. Pringle* (1986), the Court of Appeal placed great emphasis on the "hostility" of the contact, thus adopting the words of Holt C.J. in *Cole* as the proper test to be followed. In that case, the plaintiff, as a practical joke, pulled the defendant's schoolbag from his shoulder, causing the defendant to fall and injure himself. The Court held that in order for the touching to be considered a battery, it must be established that the touching is "something in the nature of overt hostility." In *F. v. West Berkshire Health Authority* (1990), the House of Lords refused to adopt the approach taken by the Court of Appeal in *Wilson*. Lord Goff highlighted the inadequacy of such an approach in the following passage:

> A prank that gets out of hand, an over-friendly slap on the back, surgical treatment by a surgeon who mistakenly thinks that the patient has consented to it, all these things may transcend the bounds of lawfulness, without being characterised as hostile ...

McMahon & Binchy (2000, p.620), on examining the differing approaches adopted in other jurisdictions to this issue, have concluded that:

> [w]hichever of these approaches is to be adopted by our courts, it is clear that a certain leeway should be given to persons in the ordinary day-to-day contacts of contemporary life: thus, no liability will normally attach for bumping into other pedestrians on a crowded footpath or touching them during an amicable conversation, or when playing sport.

As in all cases of trespass to the person, the action must arise as a consequence of the direct act of the defendant. The requirement of directness will be satisfied even if the result is achieved by some other intervening act. In *DPP v. K.* (1990), the defendant, a school pupil, had taken sulphuric acid from his chemistry class, which he poured into a hand dryer in the school bathroom in an effort to hide it. The defendant was found guilty of assault occasioning actual bodily harm when another student later used the dryer and was badly burned by the acid. Similarly, in *Scott v. Shepherd* (1773), the defendant threw some fireworks into a crowded marketplace. The fireworks, which were picked up and thrown away by persons in the marketplace, exploded and injured the plaintiff. The defendant was found to be the direct cause of the plaintiff's injuries and was therefore liable.

The intention to commit the act of battery need not exist at the commencement of the act, provided it is formed while the act is still continuing. In *Fagan v. Commissioner of Metropolitan Police* (1969), the defendant unintentionally stopped his car on a policeman's foot. When asked to move his car, he deliberately delayed in doing so and was found guilty of battery, because his later intention to inflict unlawful force was directed to a continuing act.

13.3 Assault

The definition of assault in law is different to the meaning attached to it in everyday vernacular. An assault may be committed where there is no physical contact between the plaintiff and the defendant. A party is liable where he intimates to another that he is about to inflict unlawful force on that person, leading that person to reasonably believe that he will immediately do so (*Dullaghan v. Hillen* (1957)). The tort is actionable *per se* and was described in *Kline v. Kline* (1902) as "a touching of the mind, not the body."

The tort of assault is very much of a psychological nature. Its essence is that the plaintiff has a reasonable belief that the defendant is about to inflict a battery on his person. There can be no assault if the plaintiff does not apprehend the battery, for example, where he is struck from behind (*Gambriell v. Caparelli* (1974)). Fleming (1998, p.32) has noted that it is not necessary that the plaintiff is frightened by the threat: "[i]t is sufficient if the threat would have aroused an expectation of physical aggression in the mind of a reasonable person not afflicted with exaggerated fears or a peculiar and abnormal timidity." The reasonable belief of the victim is central to the action. Thus, in *R. v. St. George* (1890), the defendant was deemed to have committed an assault where he pointed an unloaded gun at another who believed it to be loaded.

In the U.S. case of *McCraney v. Flanagan* (1980), the plaintiff alleged that the defendant had assaulted her by having sexual intercourse with her without her consent. The plaintiff could not remember the intercourse. The court held that the defendant was not guilty of assault in such circumstances, stating:

> The tort of assault occurs when a person is put in apprehension of a battery and there is no evidence here that the plaintiff feared, or even knew that such a contact might occur .... Since the interest involved is a mental one of apprehension of contact, it should follow that the plaintiff must be aware of the defendant's act at the time ...

The defendant must be in a position in which to immediately carry out the battery. So, in *Thomas v. N.U.M.* (1985), gestures made by picketers towards workers entering premises were held not to amount to assault, where the picketers were not in a position to carry out their threats. In *Stephens v. Myers* (1830), the plaintiff and defendant were sitting at the same table at a meeting in a parish hall. There were a number of people seated between them. During the meeting, the defendant became agitated and a motion was carried requesting him to leave. At this point, the defendant threatened the plaintiff and moved towards him with his fist clenched, but the defendant was stopped just short of reaching the plaintiff. It was held that the defendant had committed an assault, because the plaintiff reasonably believed that a battery would be committed, even though the intervention of a third party had prevented its occurrence. Tindal C.J. made the following direction to the jury:

> It is not every threat, when there is no actual personal violence that constitutes an assault, there must, in all cases, be the means of carrying the threat into effect. The question that I shall leave to you will be,

whether the defendant was advancing at the time, in a threatening attitude, to strike the chairman so that his blow would almost immediately have reached the chairman, if he had not been stopt; then, though he was not near enough at the time to have struck him, yet if he was advancing with that intent, I think it amounts to an assault in law. If he was so advancing, that, within a second or two of time, he would have reached the plaintiff, it seems to me it is an assault in law. If you think he was not advancing to strike the plaintiff, then only can you find for the defendant; otherwise you must find it for the plaintiff, and give him such damages, as you think the nature of the case requires.

Initially, the courts were of the view that words in themselves could not amount to an assault. In *Mead's and Belt's Case* (1823), Holroyd J. opined that, "no words or singing are equivalent to an assault." Also, in *Dullaghan v. Hillen,* Fawsitt J. stated, "that mere words, no matter how harsh, lying, insulting and provocative they may be, can never amount in law to assault." However, where the words uttered are accompanied by acts, then an action in assault may lie. Thus, in *Read v. Coker* (1853), the defendant employer, accompanied by workmen, advised the plaintiff to leave the premises or he would, quote, "wring his neck." It was held that those words amounted to an assault when considered in light of the surrounding circumstances.

In *R. v. Ireland* (1998), a House of Lords decision, the defendant's conviction for assault occasioning bodily harm was upheld in circumstances where he made phone calls to a number of different women but remained silent when they answered. On the issue of whether words could amount to an assault, Lord Steyn said:

> The proposition that a gesture may amount to an assault, but that words can never suffice, is unrealistic and indefeasible. A thing said is also a thing done. There is no reason why something said should be incapable of causing an apprehension of immediate personal violence, e.g. a man accosting a woman in a dark alley saying, "Come with me or I will slap you." I would therefore, reject the proposition that an assault can never be committed by words.

It is submitted that the approach taken by the House of Lords in *R v. Ireland* is correct. If the gist of the action is the touching of another's mind, then threatening phone calls (where the victim is unaware of the caller's exact whereabouts) could give rise to a reasonable belief that a battery is about to be committed, particularly in the modern age when the use of mobile phones is widespread. Lord Steyn stated that the silent caller:

... [i]ntends by his silence to cause fear and he is so understood. The victim is assailed by uncertainty about his intentions. Fear may dominate her emotions, and it may be the fear that the caller's arrival at her door may be imminent. She may fear the possibility of immediate personal violence.

It is clear that words may negative actions which would otherwise be considered an assault. In *Tuberville v. Savage* (1669), the plaintiff and defendant were involved in an argument. The defendant placed his hand on his sword and said "if it were not assize time, I would not take such language from you." The defendant was found not guilty of assault as his words were held to neutralise the threat.

13.4 False imprisonment

False imprisonment consists of the wrongful deprivation of personal liberty. Fawsitt J., in *Dullaghan v. Hillen*, defined the tort in the following terms:

> False imprisonment is the unlawful and total restraint of the personal liberty of another whether by constraining him or compelling him to go to a particular place or confining him in a prison or police station or private place or by detaining him against his will in a public place. The essential element offence is the unlawful detention of the person, or the unlawful restraint on his liberty .... There may be an effectual imprisonment without walls of any kind. The detainer must be such as to limit the party's freedom of motion in all directions. In effect, imprisonment is a total restraint of the liberty of the person. The offence is committed by mere detention without violence.

The restraint on liberty must be absolute. Thus, a person is falsely imprisoned where there are no other reasonable means of egress available to him. In *Bird v. Jones* (1845), the defendants blocked one side of Hammersmith Bridge to form a grandstand for a boat race. This prevented the plaintiff's desired passage, although he could have proceeded by an alternative route. He remained in the enclosure for some time and refused to cross by the opposite path. The High Court held that since the plaintiff had reasonable means of leaving the enclosure/bridge, it could not be said that he had been falsely imprisoned. Patteson J. stated that no action arose where:

> ... one man merely obstructs the passage of another in a particular direction, whether by threat of personal violence or otherwise, leaving him at liberty to stay where he is, or to go in any other direction if he pleases ...

It is clear from the decision in *Dullaghan* that false imprisonment can occur "without walls of any kind." In *Philips v. G.N. Rwy. Co. Ltd* (1903), a passenger was wrongly suspected of travelling on a train without the correct fare. Upon arriving at her destination, she was followed off the train by the ticket collector. He approached her as she ordered a cab and asked her not to leave the station. A short while later, the stationmaster arrived and, following a brief conversation, the plaintiff left in the taxicab. The plaintiff failed in her action for false imprisonment, with Lord O'Brien L.C.J. commenting that there was no evidence that she was:

> ... so dominated by the action of the ticket-collector that, succumbing to that domination, she lost her liberty. Her intended means of egress were interfered with, but she plainly could have left the station, and ... there was not "a total restraint of the liberty of the person".

In some circumstances, it may be reasonable for the detainer to impose certain conditions on the means of the plaintiff's egress, and a failure to release in breach of those conditions will not amount to false imprisonment. For example, in *Herd v. Weardale Steel Coal & Coke Co. Ltd* (1915), the plaintiff, a miner in breach of his contract of employment, had refused to continue working in the mine and demanded that he be returned to the surface. The mine owner refused to lift the plaintiff from the mine until such time as his shift had ended (which was the time when the cage for lifting the workers out would be normally available). The mine owner was held not liable for false imprisonment, because the plaintiff, as part of his contract of employment had consented to the conditions of his confinement and was bound by them.

False imprisonment does not require evidence that the plaintiff was aware of his confinement (*Murray v. Ministry of Defence* (1988)). In *Dullaghan v. Hillen*, Fawsitt J. confirmed this view, observing that:

> The fact that a person is not actually aware that he is being imprisoned does not amount to evidence that he is not imprisoned, it being possible for a person to be imprisoned in law, without his being conscious of the fact and appreciating the position in which he is being placed, laying hands upon the person of the party imprisoned not being essential.

Conversely, the plaintiff may succeed in an action for false imprisonment where he reasonably perceives himself to be wrongfully detained, even though he is free to leave in fact. In *Meering v. Grahame-White Aviation Co. Ltd* (1920), an employee of the defendant company was suspected of theft. As part of the investigation, he agreed to wait in a room with two security officers. Although he was free to leave at any time, this fact was not made known to him. Atkins L.J. in the Court of Appeal decided that, in the circumstances, a false imprisonment had taken place. However, in *Murray v. Minister for Defence* (1988), a decision of the House of Lords, Lord Griffiths noted that where "a person is unaware that he has been falsely imprisoned and has suffered no harm, he can normally expect to recover no more than nominal damages."

13.5 Defences

13.5.1 Self defence

The general principle is that a person is entitled to use reasonable force to protect his person or property. The force used must be commensurate with that which provoked it (*Dullaghan v. Hillen* (1957)). In *Gregan v. O'Sullivan* (1937), the plaintiff, a 65-year-old man, struck the defendant on the lip. In response, the younger man stabbed the plaintiff 13 times with a pitchfork and broke his arm. Not surprisingly, the defendant's claim of self defence did not succeed. On the issue of the lack of proportionality of the response, Byrne J. commented: "I am inclined to agree we ought not to weigh a method of self-defence on too fine a scales but steam hammers ought not to be used to crush flies."

It is also clear that in certain circumstances it is permissible to "get the retaliation in first", in an effort to defend oneself. In *Chaplin of Gray's Inn Case* (1400), it was stated that a person threatened with assault is "not bound to wait until the other has given a blow, for perhaps it will come too late afterwards."

13.5.2 Consent

No action for trespass to the person can lie where the plaintiff has consented to the invasion of their bodily integrity. In the words of Palles C.B. in *Hegarty v. Shine* (1878), "[i]t is indisputable that an act cannot be an assault unless it be against the will of the person assaulted." In that case, the plaintiff sued the defendant for battery based on circumstances where he had caused her to contract venereal disease. Her claim failed because she was deemed to have consented to the act of sexual intercourse, notwithstanding that she had no knowledge that he was a carrier.

Silence may amount to consent in certain situations. For example, in *O'Brien v. Cunard SS Co* (1891), it was held that the plaintiff, by stand-

ing in line and holding out her arm, had consented to receiving a vacci-
nation jab.

The consent given must be genuine and cannot be vitiated. Therefore, in *R. v. Williams* (1923), it was held that there was no valid consent given where a woman was told that having sexual intercourse with
her singing teacher was good therapy for her voice.

An action in trespass to the person will lie, notwithstanding that the
plaintiff has consented to the contact, if the consent is exceeded. In
Corcoran v. W & R Jacobs (1945), the plaintiff was an employee of the
defendant and as part of his terms and conditions of employment he
could be searched by security personnel. The Supreme Court held, that
this consent did not justify a security guard lunging at the employee
while attempting to search him.

Sports players have been held to consent to contact inherent in the
activity. So, in *Simms v. Leigh Rugby Football Club* (1969), the plaintiff's action failed where he broke his leg when tackled. It was held that
the tackle was of a kind to be expected of the sport and therefore the
plaintiff was deemed to have consented to it. However, it should be
noted that where the contact involves a serious and intentional breach
of the rules, then the defence of consent does not apply (*McNamara v.
Duncan* (1971)).

The issue of consent becomes particularly pertinent in the context of
medical procedures. It is clear that where a patient's consent has not
been obtained for a medical procedure, an action in trespass may lie.
However, where the defendant fails to fully advise the plaintiff as to the
possible consequences of the treatment (informed consent), then an
action will lie in negligence and not trespass. In *Walsh v. Family Planning Services Ltd* (1992), O'Flaherty J. explained that:

> If there had been ... a failure to give a warning as to possible future
> risks that would not involve the artificial concept of an assault, but,
> rather, a possible breach of the duty of care giving rise to a claim in
> negligence. A claim of assault should be confined to cases where
> there is no consent to the particular procedure and where it is feasible
> to look for consent.

The capacity of minors to consent to medical treatment has now been
clarified and put on a statutory footing. Under section 23 of the Non-
Fatal Offences Against the Person Act 1997, any minor who has
attained the age of 16 years or older is capable of giving a valid consent
to any surgical, medical or dental treatment.

13.5.3 Lawful authority

A person may have his liberty restrained under law. Pursuant to section 4 of the Criminal Law Act 1997, any person may arrest without warrant any person who is or who he suspects with reasonable cause to be in the act of committing an arrestable offence. At common law, while a private individual was entitled to use force to prevent the commission of a felony or to arrest a person reasonably suspected of having committed a felony, if it transpired that no felony had in fact been committed that person would be liable for false imprisonment and/or battery.

In *Humphries v. O'Connor*, although the removal of an orange lily from the plaintiff's coat was deemed to be an act of battery, it was held to be a good defence that the act was done to preserve the public peace.

13.5.4 Necessity

In certain circumstances, what would ordinarily be deemed a trespass will not be considered such where the contact was urgent and necessary. McMahon & Binchy (2000, p.642) have commented that "[t]he scope of the defence of necessity in respect of trespass to the person is uncertain. The authorities are either very old, controversial or not directly on the point." Under English law, the defence of necessity was accepted in *F v. West Berkshire Health Authority* (1990), which concerned the sterilisation of a mentally disabled woman. She had not consented to the treatment. However, Lord Goff felt that the intervention was justified on the basis that it was necessary.

13.5.5 Reasonable chastisement

A parent may only use reasonable force when disciplining a child. However, the impending adoption of the European Convention on Human Rights into Irish law could have an influence on this area of law. Article 3 of the Convention prohibits inhuman or degrading treatment or punishment and this may include physical punishment of a child (*A v. United Kingdom* (1998)).

Further reading

McMahon & Binchy, *Law of Torts* (Butterworths, 2000), pp. 615–652; Quill, *Torts in Ireland* (Gill & Macmillian, 1999), pp. 157–161; Fleming, *The Law of Torts* (LBC, 1998), pp. 21–44; Weir, *A Casebook on Tort* (Sweet & Maxwell, 2000), pp. 325–351.

14. LIABILITY FOR DEFECTIVE PRODUCTS

14.1 Introduction

This area of tort law deals with the liability of the producer of a defective product for injury caused by that product. Liability for injury of this kind was initially governed by the common law. An aggrieved party was entitled to sue on the contract he entered into with the producer or, if no such contract existed, he could sue the producer in tort law for the damage caused by the producer's negligence. The liability of a producer of a negligently produced product for damage suffered by an ultimate consumer was established on the basis of the parties' proximity or neighbourhood in *Donoghue v. Stevenson* (1932).

The protection afforded to those who suffer injury caused by defective products was further strengthened with the creation of a statutory regime of strict liability in the form of the Liability for Defective Products Act 1991.

14.2 Common law liability

Prior to Lord Atkin's seminal judgment in *Donoghue v. Stevenson* (1932), a contractual relationship was a prerequisite for establishing common law liability for injuries caused by defective products. The contract between the consumer and the producer governed the extent of the latter's liability. The doctrine of privity of contract excluded this avenue of redress for many victims such as Mrs Donoghue, whose friend purchased the defective ginger beer from the proprietor of the Wellmeadow Café. The proprietor, in turn, had purchased it from Stevenson, the producer of the product. Thus, it can be seen how a product could reach the consumer not via a contract of sale but, for example, by way of a gift, thereby depriving the consumer of a contractual remedy.

Donoghue is the most celebrated case in product liability law and provides those who suffer injury caused by such products with a method of redress notwithstanding the absence of privity of contract. Despite the fact that there was no direct contractual relationship between the producer and the plaintiff (thereby precluding an action based on contract), Lord Atkin found that the producer owed Mrs Donoghue a duty of care. Liability was imposed on the basis of the now famous "neighbour principle". This obligation was expressed in the following terms:

> ... a manufacturer of products, which he sells in such a form as to show that he intends them to reach the ultimate consumer in the form in which they left him, with no reasonable possibility of intermediate examination, and with the knowledge that the absence of reasonable care in the preparation or putting up of the products will result in an injury to the consumer's life or property, owes a duty to the consumer to take that reasonable care.

Therefore an obligation was established on the part of producers to take reasonable care to ensure that their products do not injure the ultimate consumer. In *Donoghue,* it was held to be reasonably foreseeable that the negligent production of the ginger beer would cause damage to the ultimate consumer (a person in a proximate relationship with the producer) and as a result the consumer was entitled to recover against the producer for the damage caused.

Subsequent decisions have expanded the scope of the duty of care owed at common law. For example, in *Power v. Bedford Motor Co.* (1959), the Court held that the duty of care also extended to those making repairs to the product where it was foreseeable that a want of care in the work could cause injury. In the unfortunate case of *Brown v. Cotterill* (1934), liability was imposed on a stonemason where he negligently erected a tombstone which collapsed and injured a little girl placing flowers on her grandmother's grave. In the case of *Keegan v. Owens* (1953), it was held that a supplier of swing boats for a charity event was under a duty to ensure that the person operating the swing boats was not injured by defects in the product.

14.2.1 To whom is the duty owed?

The duty owed is expansive and may be relied upon by parties other than the ultimate consumer. In *Barnett v. H & J Packer & Co Ltd* (1940), a manufacturer of sweets was held liable to a confectioner who was injured by a piece of metal protruding from one of the sweets while placing it in a display tray. The product had not reached the consumer, yet the Court found that the manufacturer was liable for his negligence. In *Stennett v. Hancock* (1939), a repairer was found liable for the negligent repair of a lorry wheel. The negligent work caused the flange of the wheel to become detached while the vehicle was in motion, thereby injuring a nearby pedestrian.

14.2.2 The duty to warn

It is important to note that the duty to take reasonable care in this regard is also extended to instructions for proper use of the product. An otherwise safe product may be highly dangerous if used in a way not intended by the producer. For example, the producers of a chemical weedkiller may be liable to the user who suffers respiratory damage for failing to warn him that inhalation of the product could be dangerous, if such damage or injury was a reasonably foreseeable consequence of their failure to warn the user. The rationale for attaching warnings to certain products was explained by the Supreme Court in *O'Byrne v. Gloucester* (1988), where the Court found that the manufacturer of a cotton skirt was liable in negligence for failing to attach a warning to the garment that the material was highly flammable. The plaintiff was severely burned when the skirt, which she was wearing at the time of the accident, came into contact with the flame from a gas heater in her home. Finlay C.J. stated that:

> Having regard to the nature of the risk involved in this particular dangerous aspect of this material, namely, major physical injury to the wearer, which was a danger foreseeable by the defendants, and having regard to the simplicity of the precaution which it is alleged the defendants should have taken, namely, the attaching to the garment of a simple warning that it was dangerous if exposed to a naked flame and would burn rapidly ... this was a precaution which a reasonably careful manufacturer and vendor of this type of clothing should have taken.

It is clear, therefore, that a manufacturer of a product may be liable under the common law where misuse of that product causes injury, provided it was reasonably foreseeable to the producer that the product could have been misused in this manner. Generally, this duty will be discharged where the producer attaches a label to the product warning the user of the dangers of misusing the product.

14.2.3 Defects in quality

Historically, Irish courts restricted the application of the principles relating to the liability of producers of defective products (as enunciated in *Donoghue*) to damage caused to persons or property other than the product itself. So how may an aggrieved party seek redress for financial loss suffered in purchasing a faulty product? The law of contract may provide the first opportunity for redress. However, if for some reason the consumer is precluded from enforcing a contractual right against the producer, *e.g.* because the product was purchased for the consumer by a friend, as in *Donoghue*, then the consumer may seek to establish the producer's tortious liability.

Defective products, like defective premises, may contain dangerous or non-dangerous defects. Non-dangerous defects diminish the value of the product in question but do not pose a threat to the consumer's life or property. Such defects are therefore are categorised as a form of economic loss and therefore not recoverable (see Chapter 4). In the words of McMahon J. in *Colgan v. Connolly Construction Co. (Ireland) Ltd* (1980): "The obligation of the builder or manufacturer in regard to the quality of his product is, in my view, something which ought to rest in contract only."

The view of the courts to such forms of loss appeared to change with the much-maligned House of Lords' decision in *Junior Books Ltd v. Veitchi* (1982). This case concerned the defendant's liability for a negligently laid concrete floor in circumstances where there was no contract between the parties. Although the defendant's negligence caused the plaintiffs considerable financial loss while the factory was closed to allow remedial work to be carried out, the loss was clearly non-dangerous in nature. Nonetheless, the House of Lords found that the loss of profits suffered by the plaintiff was recoverable. In delivering the judgment for the majority, Lord Roskill laid great emphasis on the unique relationship between the parties, which he described as being just "short of actual privity of contract" due to, *inter alia,* the plaintiff's reliance on the defendant's specialist skill in floor construction and the fact that the defendant as nominated subcontractor must have known that the plaintiff was relying on their supposed expertise.

The importance of *Junior Books* has been diminished in English law following decisions such as *Muirhead v. Industrial Tank Specialities Ltd* (1986) and *D & F Estates v. Church Commissioners for England* (1988) where Goff L.J. and Lord Bridge respectively distinguished *Junior Books* from the facts of the cases before them by laying particular emphasis on the close relationship between the parties in that case.

However, Irish courts have traditionally provided a warmer reception for the expansive doctrine set out by Lord Roskill in *Junior Books.* For example, in *Ward v. McMaster and Louth County Council* (1985), Costello J. (in the High Court, affirmed on appeal to the Supreme Court) found the defendants liable for loss caused to the plaintiff purchaser by non-dangerous (or qualitative) defects in the property.

The repercussions of the recent Supreme Court decision in *Glencar Exploration v. Mayo County Council* (2001) were explored in detail in Chapter 3 at 3.5.1. However, it may be restated at this point that Keane C.J.'s decision included an express reservation as to whether the principles enunciated by the House of Lords in *Junior Books* to determine the recoverability of damages for economic loss should be followed in this jurisdiction. Clearly, a retreat from *Junior Books* could signal the death knell for the Irish courts' willingness to award damages for loss caused by non-dangerous defects in products and premises.

14.3 Statutory liability

While the tort of negligence extended the range of liability owed by the producer of a defective product beyond the boundaries of privity of contract, it was in itself somewhat limited. The requirement of establishing the existence of a duty of care, and a consequent breach of that duty which causes damage could – in some cases – prove too high a hurdle for a potential litigant. A regime of strict (or no-fault) liability in relation to defective products was introduced into Irish law in the form of the Liability for Defective Products Act 1991. The legislation was drafted in order to implement E.C. Council Directive 85/374 on Product Liability and was intended to offer greater protection to the consumer by providing that where a defect in a product caused injury to a person, the producer was liable irrespective of whether he was at fault for the defect.

The distinguishing feature between liability under negligence and strict liability is the absence of the requirement of fault. Strict liability requires a far more exacting standard of the defendant than negligence. Under the tort of negligence, the defendant must simply maintain a standard of reasonable care. Where liability is strict, a legal duty will be imposed irrespective of whether reasonable care had been taken.

The adoption of a strict liability regime in the area of defective products law has been the subject of much academic discourse (Stapleton, *Products Liability* (Butterworths, 1994)), and in the U.S. case of *Escola v. Coca-Cola Bottling Co of Fresno* (1944), Traynor J. justified the imposition of such liability as follows:

> ... public policy demands that responsibility be fixed wherever it will most effectively reduce the hazards to life and health inherent in defective products that reach the market. It is evident that the manufacturer can anticipate some hazards and guard against the recurrence of others, as the public cannot ... If such products do nevertheless find

their way into the market it is in the public interest to place the responsibility for whatever injury they may cause upon the manufacturer, who, even if he is not negligent in the manufacture of the product, is responsible for its reaching the market.

The shift from fault-based liability to no-fault liability is intended to favour the consumer who is typically the commercially weaker party in such transactions. The introduction of strict liability attempts to redress this imbalance by ensuring the "fair apportionment of the risks inherent in modern technological production" (Recital no. 2 of E.C. Directive 85/374) between the parties.

14.3.1 The Liability for Defective Products Act 1991

Section 2(1) of the 1991 Act introduced the concept of strict liability to the field of defective products law. It provides that "the producer shall be liable in damages in tort for damage caused wholly or partly by a defect in his product." However liability under the Act is not absolute and has been somewhat diluted by the introduction of a number of defences under section 6 which, if successfully invoked, have the effect of reintroducing the element of fault into the legislation.

To successfully maintain an action under the Act, the consumer must prove that:

(i)   the product was defective;

(ii)   he suffered damage;

(iii) the defect caused the damage;

(iv)   the defendant was the "producer" of the product.

Section 11 of the Act focuses on the condition of the product rather than the conduct of the producer. It will be no defence for the producer to show that he had taken reasonable steps to prevent the injury.

The Act broadens the avenues of redress available to a party injured by a defective product. Section 11 provides that the Act "shall not affect any rights which an injured person may have under any enactment or under any rule of law." Therefore, the legislation does not replace the common law and the injured party may still bring an action on foot of a contract or under negligence depending on the circumstances of the particular case.

14.3.1.1 Who is liable?

The definition of "producer" is very broad and is not limited to the party who created the product. Under section 2(2) of the Act, a "producer" means:

(i)   a manufacturer of the product;

(ii) a producer of any raw material or component part of the product;

(iii) any person importing the product into the European Union in the course of business;

(iv) any person who held himself out to be a producer of the product by putting his name, trademark, etc., on the product;

(v)   a supplier of the product in some cases where the producer cannot be identified.

The Act recognises as a "producer" any person who is primarily responsible for exposing the public to the defective product in question. This definition obviously includes the manufacturer of the product. However, the legislation embodies a recognition that, in the modern commercial world, it may not always be practical or appropriate to attach blame to the original producer, who may not be primarily responsible for the product's mass distribution to the public. Thus, the definition is deliberately broad so as to also include any person holding himself out as the producer (*e.g.* through branding), or any person who imports such goods into the European Union, for example.

When the E.C. Directive on Product Liability was introduced, organic or primary agricultural products (including products of the soil, of stock-farming and of fisheries and game) were excluded from the ambit of the legislation. Only primary argicultural products that underwent "initial processing" were deemed to come within the parameters of the Act.

Difficulties that arose in defining the phrase "initial processing" have now been resolved with the introduction of the European Directive 1999/34/EEC. As a result, all agricultural products, regardless of how they are produced, will come within the scope of the legislation and will not be granted special dispensation because of their origin.

The Act ensures that a user who suffers damage as the result of a defect in a product will not be deprived of a remedy simply because the product was manufactured outside the European Union. The legislation provides that the first importer of the product into the Union will be deemed to be the producer for the purposes of section 2(2). This provision highlights once again the intention of the legislature to attach liability to the person who was primarily responsible for exposing the public to the defective product in question.

Section 2(3) provides that a supplier will be made liable if it is not possible to identify the producer having undertaken reasonable steps to do so. Liability will be imposed on the supplier where:

(i)   the injured person requests the supplier to identify the "producer";

(ii) a request is made within a reasonable time after the injury occurs;

(iii) the supplier fails to identify the "producer" within a reasonable time.

The inclusion of this provision is calculated to assist the plaintiff who cannot readily identify the producer of a defective product. By making the supplier potentially liable, the plaintiff will obtain redress even if the producer cannot, or does not want to be identified. The imposition of liability in this fashion will encourage retailers and other suppliers to keep comprehensive records of all their goods and will discourage them from dealing with the "less than reputable" producer, all of which should be to the ultimate benefit of the consumer.

Finally, it can be said that this provision is not too onerous, because the supplier – even where the producer is not identifiable – can discharge his obligations under section 2(3) by providing the plaintiff with details of how he came into possession of the product. In such cases, liability will move along the chain of distribution before finally resting with the original producer, or with the supplier who cannot provide proper information on the product's origins.

14.3.1.2 Damage

Section 1(1) of the 1991 Act defines the type of damage recoverable in an action for injury caused by a defective product. The Act allows for recovery where the product causes death or personal injury. The legislation further provides that "loss of, damage to, or destruction of, any item of property other than the defective product itself" may be recoverable. Recovery for defects in the quality of the product, *i.e.* non-dangerous defects is excluded.

Recovery is limited to damage caused by a product which is ordinarily intended, and is used, for private consumption. It was not the intention of the legislature that the Act should provide a means of redress to commercial enterprise. Finally, section 3 provides that claims below

IR£350 (€444) cannot be recovered under the Act, and only the excess can be recovered in claims for over IR£350.

14.3.1.3 Defective product

Under the definition provided by section 5 of the Act, a product is only defective where "it fails to provide the *safety* which a person is entitled to expect." Defectiveness is therefore defined in terms of safety and not quality. Under the legislation, one can produce a product, which may not be of the highest quality, but if it is "safe" for the purposes of the Act, no action may be maintained. Quill (1999, p.132) comments that this:

> ... is a novel feature of the legislation, in that it defines the concept of deficiency from the perspective of consumer expectation, whereas the tort of negligence focuses on the ability of the producer to foresee dangers arising from the product and to take measures to alleviate such dangers. In practice these two perspectives may lead to the same result in many instances, but the shift in focus certainly appears to be pro-plaintiff, making the consumer's expectations the central point of concern, rather than one of a number of competing considerations in determining whether the product is defective.

It is also important to note that the 1991 Act specifies that the product must of a standard of safety that the person is *entitled* to expect. As has been commented earlier in this chapter, some products by their very nature will always be unsafe, *e.g.* a lawnmower, and to render them completely safe may be impractical or impossible. In determining what standard of safety the user is entitled to expect, regard must be had to all the surrounding circumstances, including:

(i)   the presentation of the product;

(ii)   the use to which it was expected the product would be put;

(iii)   the time when the product was put into circulation.

The presentation of the product is critical in determining the safety a person is entitled to expect. The use to which it is reasonably expected that the product would be put is also very important in determining safety. The producer cannot be expected, nor does the Act require, that the producer guarantee the safety of the product no matter how it is used, *e.g.* a person is not entitled to expect that a carving knife could be used safely as a razor. However, the inclusion of the words "the use to which it could reasonably be expected that the product would be put" implies that a producer shall be liable even where that product is misused, if that misuse could be reasonably expected.

It would seem therefore that the producer of a powerful adhesive for example, would be under an obligation to label the item in question with a warning of the dangers of inhaling the fumes from such a product. In this way, it can be seen that the Act mirrors the common law position in relation to the obligation of the producer to warn users about the dangers of misusing the product, and reflects the fact the concept of reasonable foreseeability (a notion more familiar to negligence) has not been completely dispensed with.

Finally, regard must be had under the legislation for the time the product was put into circulation. Certainly, a person is not entitled to expect that a chocolate cake for example, will be fit for consumption three years after it has been produced. The time in which such products have been put onto the market will be very important. This circumstance would also seem to imply that the product will not be considered defective simply because another better product enters the market at a later stage.

14.3.1.4 Defences

There are a number of specific defences listed under section 6 of the Act. There can be no doubting that these defences have weakened the effectiveness of the legislation by providing the producer with a method of avoiding liability even where a person has established that the defect in the product caused him damage. These defences are as follows:

(a) Where the producer did not put the product into circulation: It will be a good defence for the producer to establish that he did not launch the product on the market. Therefore, it would seem that a worker on a factory floor would not succeed in an action under the Act where he was injured as the result of a defective product that, while completed, had not yet been circulated to the general public.

(b) Where the defect did not exist at the time the product was put into circulation: If the defect was not in existence at the time the product was under the control of the producer, then it would seem fair that liability should not attach to the producer for a defect which arises at a later date. This defence can be successfully invoked where the producer can show that his quality control mechanisms were such that it was probable that the defect did not occur while it was under his control, and therefore must have developed after it left his control. It would

appear that such a requirement is contrary to strict liability and more closely represents the principles of negligence. If the producer can establish reasonable quality controls, then he may not be liable. However, it is important to remember that if the defect was always contained within the product but did not arise until a later date, the producer may still be liable.

(c) Where the product was not manufactured for a commercial purpose: This defence would appear to be in accordance with the commercial nature of the legislation. If the product was not manufactured for a commercial purpose, liability will not attach regarding injuries caused as a result of a defect contained therein. Therefore, the helpful uncle who builds a tree house for his sister's children will not be liable under the Act where the children are injured as a result of the tree house collapsing.

(d) Where the defect is due to compliance with mandatory requirement: If the defect arose from changes made to the product as a result of the producer's attempt to comply with national or Community law, then the producer may have a good defence. Take for example, a manufacturer who produces tracksuits for children in the Irish market. Let us say for argument's sake, that in order to import the goods into the U.K., the Irish manufacturer must alter the material content of the product in order to comply with the much stricter flammability tests required under law in the U.K. Unfortunately, because of this change, the garment now causes some children to develop an allergic reaction to the clothing. Under section 6, the Irish manufacturer would have a good defence if he could establish that the defect (which caused the allergic reaction) arose from changes he had to make to his product in order to comply with the U.K. flammability tests.

While a manufacturer may not be made strictly liable under the 1991 Act where the defect has arisen due to his compliance with mandatory requirements, the possibility does exist that such a manufacturer could still be liable in negligence under the common law. In *Duffy v. Rooney and Dunnes Stores (Dundalk) Ltd* (1997), a two-year-old child was very badly burned when the coat she was wearing came into contact with an open fire. The defendants argued that the garment was not in contravention of any mandatory standards. At the time of the accident, the only guideline in place in this area was I.S. 148:1988, which dealt with the flammability of children's garments. These guidelines only applied to nightdresses and other undergarments (not coats), and were not therefore directly applicable to the case. More importantly, however, the defendants argued that it was not common practice in the industry to label such garments. The Court, in finding for the plaintiff, accepted that generally in cases of negligence against the professional man, evidence that he followed general practice in the industry would be a good defence. However, Laffoy J. pointed out that there are exceptions to this general rule. Evidence that the professional man followed common practice where that practice contained defects which should have been obvious to a person who gave the matter due consideration will not absolve him from an action in negligence. The rationale for such a rule, according to Laffoy J., was encapsulated by Henchy J.'s judgement in *Roche v. Peilow* (1985), where he stated that:

> The reason for that exception or qualification is that the duty imposed by the law rests on the standard to be expected from a reasonably careful member of the profession, and a person cannot be said to be acting reasonably if he automatically and mindlessly follows the practice of others when by taking thought he would have realised that the practice in question was fraught with peril for his client and was readily avoidable or remediable.

Thus, while a producer will not be liable for defects created as a result of his adhering to mandatory requirements, such a defence may not always be successful under the common law. If the mandatory requirements themselves contained defects which would have been obvious to the reasonable producer, then the producer will be liable where he slavishly followed such requirements.

(e) The "state of the art defence": This defence further erodes the regime of strict liability under the Act. It essentially provides that if the producer can establish that at the time the product was produced, the state of scientific and technical knowledge was not such as to enable the existence of the defect to be discovered, then the producer will not be liable. As Newdick ([1985] 47 C.L.J. 433) has commented:

> Such a defence tends to direct attention away from the alleged defect in the product and toward the conduct of the manufacturer and, therefore, approximates to a test of reasonable care in negligence.

In the *E.C. Commission v. U.K.* (1997), the European Court of Justice stated that such knowledge consisted of the most advanced state of technical knowledge available to the producer at the time.

It is notable that meeting the requirements of the "state of the art defence" will allow the producer to avoid liability under the Act and yet this may not be the case under the common law. Where a producer takes an unreasonable risk with the health of the public by putting a product into circulation which causes injury because of its defective nature, it will not be a defence for such a producer to say that the product was "safe" in accordance with the best available knowledge. If the risk was unreasonable in light of the possibility of damage and the seriousness of that possible damage, then the producer, while absolved of liability under statute, will be guilty of negligence for exposing the public to the unreasonable risk.

14.3.1.5 Contributory negligence

Under section 9(2) of the Act, the defence of contributory negligence shall apply to actions relating to defective products. McMahon & Binchy (2000, p. 295) discuss the conceptual difficulties created where the plaintiff is guilty of contributory negligence but the defendant is strictly liable. How does one apportion blame? The authors suggest that section 9(2):

> ... does not require the Court to compare the respective degrees of fault of the plaintiff and defendant. On the contrary, it envisages reduction or disallowance of the claim by virtue of a consideration of "all the circumstances" where the damage is caused by a defect in the product and the fault of the plaintiff or his proxy.

14.3.1.6 Limitation period

Section 7(1) of the Principal Act provides for a limitation period of three years in which an action must be brought. This period begins to run from the date the action accrued or the date on which the plaintiff became aware or ought reasonably to have been aware of the damage, the defect or the producer's identity.

14.4 Conclusion

It is beyond question that the introduction of the Liability for Defective Products Act 1991 has improved the lot of users of defective products under Irish law. In the first instance, the legislation does not replace, but rather complements, the range of remedies already in existence under the common law. Second, the legislation introduces a regime of strict liability whereby liability will lie without the injured party having to prove fault on the part of the producer. Finally, the definition of a "producer" is extremely broad and therefore plaintiff-friendly.

However, the dearth of reported case law since the enactment of the legislation would indicate that it has not had a revolutionary effect on product liability litigation in Ireland. Lunney & Oliphant (2000), commenting on the comparable English legislation, note that this may not be an accurate method of measuring the effectiveness of such legislation, "as the Act may play a role in encouraging producers to settle claims, especially in multi-party actions."

Further reading

McMahon & Binchy, *Law of Torts* (Butterworths, 2000), pp. 249–298; Quill, *Torts in Ireland* (Gill & Macmillian, 1999), pp. 128–136; Lunney & Oliphant, *Tort Law: Text and Materials* (Oxford University Press, 2000), pp. 488–500.

15. THE LIMITATION OF ACTIONS

15.1 Introduction

The law attempts to ensure the reasonably prompt determination of disputes between individuals by laying down time limits within which a cause of action must be initiated. A party attempting to initiate an action outside the limitation period is said to be "statute-barred," and as a consequence the defendant enjoys a complete defence to the plaintiff's putative claim. However, it should be noted that statute barring is merely a procedural defence, in that it must be expressly pleaded by the defendant in order to be effective (*Tuohy v. Courtney* (1994)).

In *Tuohy*, Finlay C.J. explained that the right to litigate constituted an enumerated personal right under Article 40.3.1° of the Constitution. In establishing periods of limitation for the institution of proceedings, the legislature was engaged in a balancing of constitutional rights and interests, namely balancing the right of a plaintiff to litigate against the constitutional right of a defendant to be protected against unjust or burdensome claims. Thus, the common good was best served by the existence of a procedural prohibition on delayed claims. He stated that:

> ... the purpose of statutes of limitation is to protect defendants against stale claims, to promote the expeditious trial of actions and to promote a certainty of finality in potential claims which will permit individuals to arrange their affairs whilst at the same time ensuring that the specified time limits do not unreasonably or unjustly cause hardship.

Section 11 of the Statute of Limitations 1957 provides that, as a general rule, an action in tort must be brought before the expiration of six years from the date on which the cause of action accrued. Section 11(2)(b) further provides that an action claiming damages for negligence, nuisance or breach of duty in respect of *personal injuries* to any person, shall not be brought after the expiration of *three years* from the date on which the cause of action accrued. Section 11(2)(c) applies the shorter three-year limitation period to actions for slander.

15.2 Accrual of causes of action

It is clear that the date on which the plaintiff's cause of action accrued is of central importance in determining the time period within which he must initiate his cause of action. The general rule provides that a cause of action is deemed to have accrued when the constituent elements of the tort first come into being (*Hegarty v. O'Loughran* (1990)). For this purpose, there are two distinct forms of tort. The first involves the commission of a wrongful act, which is actionable *per se*, that is without proof of actual damage. In this situation, the cause of action is deemed to have accrued and time consequently begins to run from the date on which the wrongful act is committed. Examples of torts which are actionable *per se* include libel and trespass to land. The second form of tort is actionable only on proof of actual damage, for example negligence and slander. As a consequence, time does not run against the plaintiff until some damage has actually occurred.

A particular problem in this context is that damage may occur before it is discovered. A number of questions arise for consideration. Should time run from the date upon which the plaintiff discovered the damage, or the date on which he could reasonably be expected to have discovered the damage, or should the operative date be the date on which the damage actually occurred? The traditional judicial response to this question was to hold that the limitation period began to expire as soon as the tort was committed (for wrongs actionable *per se*) or when damage accrued as a result of the commission of the tort (for wrongs actionable on proof of actual damage). This approach was considered and ultimately rejected by Carroll J. in *Morgan v. Park Developments* (1983), a case concerning the defendant's alleged liability for negligently constructing a house subsequently purchased by the plaintiff. She expressed the view that a "discoverability rule" should apply to section 11(2) of the Statute of Limitations 1957, and said it would be "indefensible in the light of the Constitution" to accept an argument that a plaintiff could have his action statute-barred before he knew he had one.

In *Hegarty v. O'Loughran* (1990), the plaintiff underwent two operations on her nose. The first, in 1973, was unsuccessful. A remedial operation took place in 1974 under a different surgeon. The plaintiff did not issue proceedings in relation to the damage caused by the first operation until 1982. In the High Court, Barron J. held that the plaintiff's action against the defendant was statute-barred. He refused to apply a "discoverability rule" to an action for damages for personal injuries. On appeal, the plaintiff argued, *inter alia*, that the Court should interpret section 11(2)(b) in a manner consistent with the provisions of the Constitution. Finlay C.J., in dismissing the plaintiff's appeal, held that her cause of action accrued at the time "when a provable personal injury, capable of attracting compensation, occurred ... which was the completion of the tort alleged to be committed against her." The then Chief Justice went on to overrule *Morgan v. Park Developments,* stating that it was not unconstitutional for the legislature to set a time limit within which a particular action had to be brought, because such a time limit represented a balance between the plaintiff's right to litigate and the defendant's interest in certainty in relation to potential liability. He stated that "to interpret [section 11(2)] as being based on discoverability, though possibly very desirable, would be to legislate."

15.3 Legislative intervention

One year after the decision in *Hegarty v. O'Loughran*, the Oireachtas passed the Statute of Limitations (Amendment) Act 1991. This Act creates a concept known as the "date of knowledge" in respect of cases where damages are claimed for *personal injuries* caused by negligence, nuisance or breach of duty. It does *not* affect the limitation period applicable in respect of claims for damage to *property*. Section 3 of the Act provides that personal injury actions arising from acts of negligence, nuisance or breach of duty may not be brought after the expiration of three years from the date on which the cause of action accrued or the date of knowledge, if later, of the person injured. Section 2 provides that references to a person's date of knowledge are references to the date on which he first had knowledge of the following facts:

(i)   that he has been injured;

(ii)   that the injury in question was significant;

(iii) that the injury was attributable in whole or in part to the act or omission which is alleged to constitute negligence, nuisance or breach of duty;

(iv)   the identity of the defendant; and

(v)   if it is alleged that the act or omission was that of a person other than the defendant, the identity of that person and the additional facts supporting the bringing of an action against the defendant.

Section 2(3) goes on to provide that a person shall not be fixed with knowledge of a fact ascertainable only with the help of expert advice so long as he has taken all reasonable steps to obtain (and, where appropriate, to act on) that advice. In *Boylan v. Motor Distributors Ltd* (1994), the plaintiff suffered injury when her finger was caught in the door of a van. She sued the owners of the van but only joined the manufacturers more than three years after her accident, having received an engineer's report which suggested that the door's design was faulty. Lynch J. held that the plaintiff was not statute-barred in these circumstances, since she had not acted unreasonably in failing to commission an engineer's report earlier. The injury suffered did not reasonably suggest that it was caused by a defect in the design of the door.

In *Gallagher v. Minister of Defence* (1998), O'Higgins J. held that knowledge for the purpose of the Statute of Limitations did not mean vague suspicion but rather a reasonable belief in a particular set of circumstances such as would justify a person in issuing legal proceedings. In this case, the plaintiff, an army bandsman, issued a plenary summons in 1993, suing the defendants for damage to his hearing, which occurred in the course of his employment. On the facts, and notwithstanding that the plaintiff had been referred for an audiogram by his superiors in 1989, it was held that his claim was not statute-barred in 1993. O'Higgins J. echoed the words of Lord Donaldson in *Halford v. Brooks* (1991):

> In this context, knowledge clearly does not mean "I know for certain and beyond possibility of contradiction". It does however mean knowing with sufficient confidence to justify embarking on the preliminaries to the issue of a writ, such as submitting a claim to the proposed defendant, taking legal or other advice, and collecting evidence. Suspicion, particularly if it is vague and unsupported will indeed not be enough, but reasonable belief will normally suffice.

In *Maguire v. Smithwick* (1997), the plaintiff alleged that the defendant negligently caused her injury in carrying out a caesarean section. Following the operation (which took place in 1987), she noticed a growth at the site of the incision. She brought the growth to the attention of her doctor, the defendant, who told her it was not a cause for concern. She returned to the defendant for a check-up some two months after the operation. The wound at the site of the incision had closed up but there was still an unsightly lump, which the defendant allegedly told her was "okay". The plaintiff initiated proceedings in 1993. Geoghegan J. had to consider the plaintiff's relevant state of knowledge at this time. He also considered at what stage did the plaintiff know that her injury was serious. He cited with approval the Court of Appeal's decision in *Broadley v. Guy Clapham & Company* (1994) where Hoffmann L.J. opined:

> I think [counsel for the respondent] was right when he said that the words "which [are] alleged to constitute negligence, nuisance or breach of duty" serve to identify the facts of which the plaintiff must have knowledge without implying that he should know that they constitute a breach of a rule, whether of law or some other code of behaviour.

Geoghegan J. noted that the presence of the lump described by the plaintiff should have informed her that her injury was significant. As a result, she was statute-barred.

In *Behan v. Bank of Ireland* (1998), the plaintiff, a farmer, claimed that his bank manager had negligently dissuaded him from selling part of his lands in 1981 when Irish agriculture was in a particularly deep recession. He claimed that he acted on foot of this negligent advice and his bank manager's assurances that he would be provided with the requisite financial support by the bank to facilitate the survival of his business through the period. As a result of his reliance on this advice, the plaintiff suffered both economic loss and personal injury but did not institute legal proceedings against the bank until 1990. The Supreme Court heard the plaintiff's appeal from Morris J.'s determination that he was statute-barred. The court considered whether time ran against the plaintiff from the date when the allegedly negligent advice was given, or the date when the plaintiff relied on the advice, or from when detriment was suffered by the plaintiff, or whether time only ran from the moment when the plaintiff became aware that the advice was bad. The Supreme Court held that by 1983 the plaintiff must have known that the advice he had received was bad, and accordingly, his cause of action arose at that date. Since more than six years had elapsed before proceeding were issued, his claim was therefore statute-barred.

The plaintiff's claim for personal injuries (based on his argument that the negligent advice led him to engage in the excessive consumption of alcohol which contributed to his nervous breakdown) was similarly statute-barred. According to Keane J., "the cause of action in this instance accrued in 1982 when the nervous breakdown occurred and, accordingly, the claim was ... statute barred at the time the plenary summons was issued."

15.4 The suspension of time

There are special provisions in the Act, which have the effect of stopping the running of time against persons who are under a disability. However, the disability, in order to be operative, must exist at the time of the accrual of the cause of action. Disability, for the purposes of the 1957 Act, encompasses those who have not reached their majority, are of unsound mind or are convicts.

There is no statutory definition of what constitutes an "unsound mind" but lack of mental capacity is conclusively presumed whenever a person is detained in any institution under any enactment authorising the detention of persons of unsound mind or lunatics. In *Kirby v. Leather* (1965), the Court of Appeal defined "a person of unsound mind" as one who, by reason of mental illness, is incapable of managing his own affairs in relation to the accident as a reasonable man would do.

With regard to the running of time against minors, the legislature initially sought to distinguish between infants in the custody of a parent when the cause of action arose and those in the custody of a guardian acting in *loco parentis*. A number of challenges were made to this distinction (*O'Brien v. Keogh* (1972), *Moynihan v. Greensmyth* (1977)). Following the Supreme Court's decision in the latter case, section 49(2)(a) of the 1957 Act was deemed to be unconstitutional. As a result, all infants are treated in the same fashion with regard to the running of time for the initiation of causes of action. Therefore, time does not begin to run until a person ceases to be under a disability. So, for example, time only runs against someone who was an infant when the accident occurred on that person reaching his majority.

The Statute of Limitations (Amendment) Act 1991 has further extended the limitation period applicable to persons under a disability who sue in respect of personal injuries. Should the plaintiff have been under a disability at the date of knowledge (as defined), time will be suspended for the duration of the period of disability. This extension is effected notwithstanding that the plaintiff was not under a disability at the date on which the cause of action accrued.

The Statute of Limitations (Amendment) Act 2000 was enacted following the settlement of Ms Sophia McColgan's action against the North Western Health Board in 1998. The plaintiff was physically and sexually abused by her father and alleged negligence on the part of agents of the Health Board in failing to discover and/or properly investigate her plight (*Irish Times*, January 23, 1998). Section 2 of the Act provides that a person shall, for the purposes of bringing an action, be under a disability while he or she is suffering from psychological injury caused by an act of sexual abuse in childhood, which is of such significance that his or her will or ability to make a reasoned decision to bring an action is substantially impaired.

Section 2 (7) goes on to define "an act of sexual abuse" as:

(i) any act of causing, inducing or coercing a person to participate in any sexual activity,

(ii) any act of causing, inducing or coercing the person to observe any other person engaging in any sexual activity, or

(iii) any act committed against, or in the presence of, a person that any reasonable person would, in all the circumstances, regard as misconduct of a sexual nature:

provided that the doing or commission of the act concerned is recognised by law as giving rise to a cause of action.

15.5 The effect of fraud

Section 71(1) of the Statue of Limitations 1957 deals with the effect of fraud on the running of time. The subsection provides that, where an action is based on the fraud of the defendant or his agents, or where the plaintiff's right of action is concealed by the act of such person, the period of limitation shall not begin to run until the plaintiff has discovered the fraud, or could with reasonable diligence have discovered it.

In *McDonald v. McBain* (1991), the plaintiff sought unsuccessfully to rely on this section. She bought a house from the defendant. Relations between them broke down and the sale was completed only by bringing a specific performance action. Soon after (March 1974), the house was burnt down. The plaintiff was aware that the defendant was at the house on the night of the fire with flammable materials. The defendant, who was under immediate suspicion, was interviewed by gardaí although no charges were preferred. In 1976, two men told the plaintiff that the defendant was responsible for the fire. However, they retracted their allegations when interviewed by gardaí. Finally, in October 1983, the defendant admitted his liability. In April 1985, the plaintiff issued a plenary summons for breach of contract, negligence and trespass. The defendant raised the Statute of Limitations in his defence. The plaintiff argued her right of action was concealed by the defendant's fraud. She said the limitation period should not run against her until she could, with reasonable diligence, have discovered the defendant's liability. Morris J. dismissed the plaintiff's claim saying that, on the evidence, she had sufficient evidence tending to prove the defendant liable to warrant her instituting proceeding within the limitation period. He held that in this case her right of action had not been concealed. Since the defendant's admission was not an essential ingredient for an action in trespass but merely went to its further proof, his non-admission within the six-year period did not operate to conceal her right of action.

In the recent case of *Heffernan v. O'Herlihy* (1998), a solicitor's failure to communicate to a client that proceedings had not been instituted on her behalf was held to constitute fraud for the purposes of the Statue of Limitations. Kinlen J. approved the decision of the English Court of Appeal in *Keane v. Victor Parsons & Company* (1973), where Lord Denning stated that fraud for the purposes of the English equivalent of the 1957 Act involved "knowing or reckless concealment of a right of action."

15.6 Special rules

15.6.1 Admiralty

A special two-year limitation period is applied for damage caused by a sailing vessel to another vessel or to persons and property on board, although this period may be extended pursuant to section 46(3) of the 1957 Act.

15.6.2 Actions against the estate of a deceased person

Actions which survive death are governed by section 9 of the Civil Liability Act 1961. Actions taken against the estate are maintainable only where they were instituted within the "relevant period" stipulated by the Statute of Limitations and were pending at the time of death, or they are instituted within the relevant limitation periods after death or within two years from the date of death, whichever period expires first. Thus, if proceedings were not commenced before death, the plaintiff is subject to a strict two-year limitation period running from death.

For fatal injury actions brought by the deceased's dependants under the 1961 Act, a limitation period of three years applies, which runs from the date of death or the "date of knowledge", whichever is later.

15.6.3 Air transport

Pursuant to section 17(1) of the Air Navigation and Transport Act 1936, a two-year limitation period is applied to accidents which occur in the course of air transport. This period applies to accidents which occur whilst on board, as well as whilst embarking or disembarking from the aircraft.

15.6.4 Liability for defective products

As noted in Chapter 14, pursuant to section 7(1) of the Liability for Defective Products Act 1991 a limitation period of three years exists. This period begins to run from the date the action accrued or the date on which the plaintiff became aware or ought reasonably to have been aware of the damage, the defect or the producer's identity. Furthermore, no right of action will be heard under the provisions of the 1991 Act upon the expiration of the period of 10 years from the date on which the producer put into circulation the actual product which caused the damage.

15.7 Judicial discretion

Notwithstanding the provisions of the statutes governing the limitation of actions, the courts retain a residual discretionary power to refuse to hear a claim initiated *within* the limitation period on the basis that the claim was not taken expeditiously with resultant prejudice to the defendant. This common law discretion is expressly preserved by section 5 of the Principal Act.

In *Toal v. Duignan* (1991), the plaintiff (who was born in 1961) claimed that he learned in the summer of 1983 that he was sterile due to an undiagnosed undescended testicle at birth. A number of defendants were sued, including his mother's doctor who attended at his birth. Proceedings were instituted within 15 months of his alleged discovery of the cause of action, but some 22 years after the conduct which allegedly caused his loss. The Supreme Court, in holding that the plaintiff was statute-barred, reiterated the courts' power to deem an action barred when, to do otherwise, would prejudice the defendant and lead to unfairness. Finlay C.J. stated that:

> ... where there is a clear and patent unfairness in asking a defendant to defend a case after a very long lapse of time between the acts com-

plained of and the trial then if that defendant has not himself contributed to the delay, irrespective of whether the plaintiff has contributed to it or not, the court may, as a matter of justice have to dismiss the action.

In the earlier decision of *O'Domhnaill v. Merrick* (1984), a more balanced approach was taken to the question of when a plaintiff's cause of action would be dismissed on discretionary grounds. Henchy J. had stated that:

> In all cases the problem of the court would seem to be to strike a balance between a plaintiff's need to carry on his or her delayed claim against a defendant and the defendant's basic right not to be subjected to a claim which he or she could not reasonably be expected to defend.

It is possible to characterise the *Toal* decision as one where the Supreme Court adopted an excessively defendant-friendly approach at the expense of victims of sleeping torts. A blameless plaintiff who initiates his action within the limitation period may find himself without remedy merely because of some perceived prejudice which would be suffered by the defendant should the action be allowed to proceed.

The Supreme Court's decision in *Primor plc v. Stokes Kennedy Crowley* (1996) introduced a degree of clarification on the circumstances where a court may dismiss a claim on discretionary grounds. Hamilton C.J.'s judgment makes clear that inordinate and inexcusable delay will not, of itself, justify dismissal unless the balance of justice requires the court to do so.

Further reading

McMahon & Binchy, *Law of Torts* (Butterworths, 2000), pp. 1203–1230; Quill, *Torts in Ireland* (Gill & Macmillian, 1999), pp. 411–421; Turner, "Overhauling the Statutory Limitation Regime" (September 14, 2001) 151 N.L.J. 1312.

16. DAMAGES

16.1 Introduction

A party who successfully takes an action in tort may have a number of remedies available to him. He may be entitled to seek an injunction to prevent the recurrence of the wrong or he may find himself entitled to take unilateral steps to ameliorate the effects of the defendant's wrongdoing (abatement). However, the remedy of damages is by far the most common remedy awarded by the courts and as such will be the focus of this chapter.

16.2 The indemnity principle

The primary purpose of awarding damages is to *compensate* the victim rather than punish the defendant. An award of damages should, in the words of Lord Scarman in *Lim Poh Choo v. Camden and Islington Area Health Authority* (1980):

> ... as nearly as possible put the party who has suffered in the same position as he would have been in if he had not sustained the wrong.

This approach is at variance with the purpose of awarding damages for breach of contract, where the object is to put the plaintiff in the position he would have been in had the contract been performed.

Damages are paid in a lump sum and on a "once and for all" basis (*Fournier v. CNR* (1927)). Thus, compensation will be awarded for all loss suffered by the plaintiff including past, present and future damage (*Fitter v. Veal* (1701)). Lord Scarman in *Lim Poh Choo,* outlined the common law position as follows:

> The award, which covers past, present and future injury and loss, must, under our law, be of a lump sum assessed at the conclusion of the legal process. The award is final; it is not susceptible to review as the future unfolds, substituting fact for estimate. Knowledge of the future being denied to mankind, so much of the award as is to be attributed to future loss and suffering (in many cases the major part of the award) will almost surely be wrong. There is really only one certainty: the future will prove the award to be either too high or too low.

The lump sum approach to the payment of damages has not been universally adopted. In some jurisdictions (such as New Zealand), a system of periodically reviewed payments is favoured. However, there seems little appetite in this jurisdiction for the development of such an approach. As Mahon & Binchy (2000, p.1136) have noted:

> The principal parties to litigation appear to prefer the present system. Insurance companies like to be able to close their books on claims at some point, rather than to have to make provision in their reserves for future payments extending indefinitely into the future. For plaintiffs, "a bird in the hand appears to be more satisfying than one in the bush", even, it seems, in countries where a choice between lump sum payments and periodical award is possible.

16.3 Types of damages

Damages may be awarded under a variety of heads, depending on the nature of the injury suffered by the plaintiff. These heads may be categorised as follows (i) contemptuous damages (ii) nominal damages (iii) compensatory damages (iv) exemplary damages.

16.3.1 Contemptuous damages

Contemptuous damages are awarded where the plaintiff has proven nothing more than the commission of a technical wrong. While the plaintiff may have been ultimately successful in his action, the court will merely award what is deemed to be a token amount (usually the smallest coin in circulation) reflecting the court's low opinion of the plaintiff's action (*Dawson v. M'Clelland (No.2)* (1899)). For example, in *Reynolds v. Times Newspapers Ltd* (1999), the award of the jury at first instance could clearly be categorised as contemptuous. In that case, it was found, as a matter of fact, that the plaintiff had been defamed by the defendant newspaper but the jury then assessed damages at nil. This award was substituted with 1p by the trial judge, an award that was overturned on appeal on the basis that the judge had misdirected the jury to such an extent that the plaintiff was denied a fair trial. It should be noted that where an award of contemptuous damages has been made, it does not necessarily follow that the plaintiff will also receive the costs of the action (*Deans v. Sheridan* (1993)).

16.3.2 Nominal damages

Nominal damages are awarded in situations where the law recognises that the plaintiff's rights have been infringed but he has not suffered actual damage. Nominal damages are generally awarded for wrongs that are actionable *per se*, *e.g.* actions for trespass or libel. Thus, as Holt C.J. commented in *Ashby v. White* (1703):

> ... if a man gives another a cuff on the ear, though it cost him nothing, no not so much as a little diachylon [a plaster], yet he shall have his action, for it is a personal injury. So a man shall have an action against another for riding over his ground, though it did him no damage: for it is an invasion of his property and the other has no right to come there.

An award of nominal damages is not intended to reflect the merit of the plaintiff's action (unlike contemptuous damages). Nominal damages do serve an important function, however, in vindicating the plaintiff's rights while at the same time not unduly burdening the defendant in financial terms for minor wrongs. In *Constantine v. Imperial Hotels Ltd* (1944), the plaintiff was a famous cricketer who was unjustifiably refused accommodation at one of the defendant's inns, although he did manage to obtain accommodation elsewhere. The Court held that the plaintiff was entitled to nominal damages of five guineas for this infringement of his rights. Similarly, in *Grealey v. Casey* (1901), the Court awarded a farthing damages where the plaintiff established a trespass to his person.

It is generally the case that where a plaintiff obtains an award of nominal damages, he will also have the costs of the action awarded in his favour. As O'Sullivan J. stated in *O'Keeffe v. Kilcullen* (1998):

> Nominal damages means a sum of money that may be spoken of but has no existence in point of quantity, the purposes of such damages being twofold, namely, either to assert a right or as a "peg" on which to hang an order for costs.

16.3.3 Compensatory damages

Compensatory damages are intended to compensate the plaintiff for the loss he has suffered as a result of the commission of a wrong against him. They may be subdivided into the following categories: general damages, special damages, aggravated damages.

16.3.3.1 General damages

General damages are those that cannot be easily quantified in monetary terms and are presumed to flow from the wrong of the defendant. As such they do not have to be specifically pleaded. Such damages are non-pecuniary or non-financial in nature. While it is the overriding purpose of damages in tort law to put the plaintiff in the position he enjoyed prior to the commission of the wrongful act, in many circumstances, no amount of money can provide proper restitution to the injured plaintiff. In the words of Fleming (1998, p.266):

> Not all the gold in the Bank of England can make good excruciating pain, loss of sight or limb or cosmetic injuries, but it may finance holidays, recreation and extra comforts.

Lord Scarman in *Lim Poh* distinguished the English courts' approach to awarding damages for pain and suffering from awards of damages for loss of amenity, stating that the courts:

> ... draw a clear distinction between damages for pain and suffering and damages for loss of amenities. The former depend on the plaintiff's personal awareness of pain, her capacity for suffering. But the latter are awarded for the fact of deprivation, a substantial loss, whether the plaintiff is aware of it or not.

General damages for non-pecuniary loss may be sub-categorised as follows: (a) damages for pain and suffering (b) damages for loss of expectation of life.

(a) Pain and suffering: General damages shall be awarded to compensate the plaintiff for any pain and suffering he has undergone as a result of the defendant's wrongful act. The pain suffered by the plaintiff is individual to him and therefore the courts use a subjective test in order to measure the amount of compensation payable. Damages for pain and suffering are awarded for the pain that the plaintiff is actually aware of, therefore, damages cannot be awarded where the plaintiff is not conscious of the pain. In the words of Lord Morris in *H. West & Son Ltd v. Shephard* (1964) (a House of Lords decision):

> If someone has been caused pain then damages to compensate for the enduring of it may be awarded. If, however, by reason of an injury someone is made unconscious either for a short or for a prolonged period with the result that he does not feel pain then he needs no monetary compensation in respect of pain because he will not have suffered it.

The Irish Supreme Court addressed the issue of the plaintiff's awareness of his plight in *Cooke v. Walsh* (1984), where medical evidence was presented that the mental age of the plaintiff (who was 11 years old at the time of the action), "would in adult life be hardly more than about two years." The majority of the Court was of the view that the fact that the plaintiff was not aware of his situation would affect the general damages awarded to him. Griffin J. commented that the award would be greater in the case of a quadriplegic who had not suffered any brain damage because such a plaintiff "is fully aware of his condition ... [and] sees himself as a prisoner for life in his wheelchair." The plaintiff in the instant case had, due to his mental incapacity, "been spared the considerable mental suffering which would follow from knowledge or appreciation of the virtual destruction of his life" and as such damages for pain and suffering would not be as great.

As the test is one of subjectivity, the reaction of the plaintiff to the injury will have an effect on the sum awarded to him. If he is of strong character and has coped well with his ill fortune, then his damages will be reduced (*Prendergast v. Joe Malone Self Drive Ltd* (1967)).

A concern about the possibility of over-generous awards to plaintiffs that could be viewed as punitive, rather than compensatory, prompted the Supreme Court to set a judicial tariff on the amount of general damages that could be awarded for pain and suffering. This tariff can be seen as an policy-driven device which artificially limits the courts' recognition of the pain and suffering endured by the plaintiff. In *Sinnott v. Quinnsworth* (1983), the Supreme Court reduced an award of damages made by the jury from £800,000 to £150,000. O'Higgins C.J. expressed the view that sums awarded "should not exceed a sum in the region of contemporary standards and money values." The notional cap placed on the award of general damages was raised to £200,000 by the High Court in *Connolly v. Bus Éireann* (1996). The cap has been raised to £250,000 in *Kealy v. Minister for Health* (1999). In that case, the plaintiff, a middle-aged lady, was infected with hepatitis as the result of being injected with a contaminated blood product. In examining the upper limit placed on general damages following *Sinnott*, Morris P. distinguished *Sinnott* from the present case on a number of grounds. First, in *Sinnott,* the overall damages awarded to the plaintiff, who was paraplegic, included large provision for loss of earnings, house renovation, etc., which did not apply to the case before him. Second, the award in *Sinnott* was made at a time of economic depression, when incomes relative to the present day were smaller.

(b) Loss of expectation of life: Under Irish law, a plaintiff is entitled to an award of damages where his life expectancy has been reduced as a result of the defendant's wrong (*Flint v. Lovell* (1934)). In light of the philosophical questions raised by this heading, all the courts can do is award an amount which is fair and reasonable. In the words of Maguire C.J. (in *McMorrow v. Knott* (1959)):

> In considering it and the other heads of damages … the jury should [be] told that it is quite impossible in a case such as this to give perfect compensation. In one sense nothing would compensate the plaintiff for the dreadful consequences of an accident for which admittedly he had no blame. A jury must, however, be just and towards this end must be reasonable in arriving at a figure.

16.3.3.2 Special damages

By contrast with general damages, special damages are those damages which are the specifically quantifiable expenses that the plaintiff has incurred as a result of the defendant's tortious act. For example, a plaintiff who was rendered paraplegic as a result of the defendant's action will have suffered losses of a pecuniary nature as a result of the accident, *e.g.* hospital bills, house renovations, carer's costs, etc. These damages are known as special damages and must be specifically pleaded. For the present purposes, special damages may be subdivided under the following heads: (a) loss of income and (b) medical expenses.

(a) Loss of income: Depending on the nature of the injury suffered by the plaintiff and his prospects for future employment, his earning capacity may be greatly affected. Walsh J. (in the Supreme Court) in *Long v. O'Brien & Cronin Ltd* (1972) outlined the factors to be considered when deciding an award for loss of income:

> Not merely is the former earning capacity of the plaintiff relevant but so also is the present physical condition, his prospective physical condition, the state of the labour market, the particular trade or skill which he has and the prospects for exercising it in the future having regard to the dimunition of his capacity to do so resulting from the injuries he has sustained.

The medical condition of the plaintiff will have obvious implications for his earning capacity. However, it should be noted that not every disability will render the plaintiff unemployable. For example, if an accountant lost an index finger in an accident, it may not affect his prospective earning capacity quite as much as it would affect a surgeon who suffered the same fate. As Walsh J. stated in *McKenna v. Meighan* (1966):

> It may well be that what can be described as a partial disability may from an economic point of view be equal to total if it prevents him from doing the only type of work available to him or may be the cause of no economic loss at all if it does not interfere with the work available to him.

The plaintiff is entitled to damages for the earnings he has lost where the length of his earning years has been reduced (*Doherty v. Bowaters Irish Wallboard Mills Ltd* (1968)).

It is clear that the plaintiff's ability to find employment following the accident will, regardless of injury, be affected by the state of the labour market. Thus, when calculating damages for loss of earnings, factors such as economic downturns, redundancy and natural ill health may reduce the amount of the award (*Reddy v. Bates* (1983)). In *Murphy v. Minister for Defence* (1999), Barron J. expressed the view that redundancy and high unemployment was a unfortunate fact of life and that when calculating damages, cognisance should be taken of the fact that it would be highly unlikely that the plaintiff would have worked every week for the rest of his working life but for the accident.

The importance of actuarial evidence cannot be over-emphasised in this area (*Sexton v. O'Keeffe* (1966)). However, the evidence of an actuary cannot contravene the ultimate issue rule. This rule precludes an expert witness from giving evidence on an issue which the court itself must determine. In the words of Walsh J. in *Swords v. St. Patrick's Copper Mines* (1966), "the actuary is not the judge of the case."

It is clear that the plaintiff's award of damages for pecuniary loss is decreased to take into account tax he would have paid on the earnings had they arisen in the normal course of his occupation (*Glover v. BLN (No. 2)* (1973) and *Cook v. Walsh* (1984)).

(*b*) *Medical expenses:* A plaintiff is entitled to the recovery of reasonable medical expenses relating to his injury. Section 2(1) of the Health (Amendment) Act 1986 permits health boards to charge for in-patient and out-patient services in respect of the treatment of certain injuries caused by the negligent use of mechanically propelled vehicles in public places. This provision ensures that it is the defendant (or his insurance company) who bears the cost of the plaintiff's medical expenses. In *O'Rourke v. Scott* (1993), Kinlen J. proposed that a maximum charge of £100 per day for a hospital stay should be recoverable from the defendant. This charge, which became known as the "Kinlen

Order", was subsequently increased to a maximum of £150 (€190.46) per day. In *Crilly v. Farrington* (2000), the Eastern Health Board submitted that the daily hospital charge should be calculated by averaging the annual cost of running the hospital divided by the number of beds available. On this basis, the daily charge for Beaumont Hospital would be approximately £525 (€666.61). In the High Court, Geoghegan J. rejected the Health Board's submission, stating that "hospital charges should be assessed strictly on a *quantum meruit* basis, not by general averaging." On appeal to the Supreme Court, Denham J. allowed the appeal of the claimant Health Board. She differed from Geoghegan J. in her interpretation of the Health (Amendment) Act 1986, holding that the calculation of hospital charges based on the average daily cost of maintaining a hospital bed was both reasonable and *intra-vires* the Act. This decision is likely to have serious repercussions for both insurers and those obliged to take out motor insurance policies alike.

Deductability of collateral benefits: Section 2 of the Civil Liability (Amendment) Act 1964 provides that when calculating damages in respect of the defendant's wrongful act that has caused injury not resulting in death, account should be taken of:

(i)   any sum payable in respect of the injury under any contract of insurance; or

(ii) any pension, gratuity or other like benefit payable under statute or otherwise in consequence of the injury.

The rationale for this provision is that the plaintiff should not benefit from donations or payouts by third parties that would have the effect of doubly compensating him for his injuries. In *Hogan v. Steele & Co.* (2000), the plaintiff, an employee of the E.S.B., had received discretionary sick leave payments from his employer following an accident with a third party. Such payments were made on the understanding that he would refund his employer from any sum of compensation received from the third party. Macken J., holding that the sums advanced should not be deducted from the damages awarded against the defendant, stressed the fact that the plaintiff had no automatic entitlement to the payments, which were:

> No more than the sum which, absent the notice party exercising a discretion to pay, and paying, would or could have been borrowed by the plaintiff from a local bank or his credit union. Such borrowings, so long as they were reasonably incurred, would undoubtedly be payable by the defendant to the plaintiff as part of the plaintiff's special damages.

By contrast, payments for sick-leave under an employee's contract of employment are deductible as they are unconditional.

16.3.3.3 Aggravated damages

Aggravated damages are compensatory in nature. Such damages are awarded where the plaintiff suffers further injury as a consequence of the manner in which the wrong was committed, the conduct of the tortfeasor after the commission of the wrong, *e.g.* a refusal to ameliorate the harm, and the conduct of the tortfeasor in the defence of his action, including the trial of the action (per Finlay C.J., *Conway v. Irish National Teachers Organisation* (1991))

This category of damages was the subject of a Law Reform Commission *Report on Aggravated, Exemplary and Restitutionary Damages* (2000) where the following definition was proposed:

> Aggravated damages are damages to compensate a plaintiff for added hurt, distress or insult caused by the manner in which the defendant committed the wrong giving rise to the plaintiff's claim, or by the defendant's conduct subsequent to the wrong, including the conduct of legal proceedings. In implementing a policy of moderation, we believe aggravated damages will only be appropriate where there has been reprehensible, high-handed behaviour on the part of the defendant and such damages should only be awarded in exceptional cases. Both because of this and because the definition given marks a divergence from at least some of the existing case law, we recommend the incorporation of this definition in legislation.

Such damages are commonly awarded in cases involving actions for defamation where, for example, the defendant refuses to withdraw or apologise for the offending statement. In *Kennedy v. Hearne* (1987), the plaintiff brought an action in defamation alleging that he had been defamed when the Revenue Commissioners continued to prosecute an action for the recovery of allegedly unpaid taxes after he had paid the due amount. The plaintiff who was successful in his action, was awarded £10,000 in aggravated damages in recognition of the defendant's unjust attack on his reputation during the course of the trial. Finlay C.J. justified the award in the following terms:

> Having regard to what I would consider the very large difference between the seriousness of the original defamation and the much greater seriousness of the harm to the plaintiff's character and reputation as a solicitor arising from the conduct of the proceedings in the High Court, I conclude that the sum of £2,000 as aggravated damages was significantly inadequate to compensate as a solicitor for being

publicly accused in the city in which he practises, of being a cheat and having no reputation. In those circumstances, I am satisfied that this Court should intervene on this appeal to adjust those damages, and I would substitute for the sum of £2,000 aggravated damages a sum of £10,000 aggravated damages, making a total award of damages for defamation £10,500.

16.3.4 Exemplary damages

Exemplary damages are not compensatory in nature but rather are designed to punish or make an example of the defendant for his behaviour. The award of exemplary damages reflects the court's abhorrence of the defendant's conduct. In *Conway v. Irish National Teachers Organisation* (1991), Finlay C.J. stated that such damages:

> ... are intended to mark the court's particular disapproval of the defendant's conduct in all the circumstances of the case and its decision that it should publicly be seen to have punished the defendant for such conduct by awarding such damages, quite apart from its obligation, where it may exist in the same case, to compensate the plaintiff for the damage which he or she has suffered.

As outlined in Chapter 1, it is the principal purpose of the law of torts to compensate the plaintiff for the wrong he has suffered. Therefore, exemplary damages, which are punitive in nature, do not rest easily within the realm of tort law. As the assignation of guilt (and punishment) is the function of our criminal justice system, the civil courts have been reticent to award exemplary damages save in the most exceptional of circumstances. In *Rookes v. Barnard* (1964), the House of Lords recognised the importance of placing a restriction on the circumstances when such damages should be awarded. In that case it was held that exemplary damages should only be awarded in the following situations: (i) cases of oppressive, arbitrary or unconstitutional action by the servants of government; (ii) cases where the defendant's conduct was calculated to make a profit in excess of the compensation ordinarily recoverable by the plaintiff; and (iii) cases expressly authorised by statute.

The categories as developed in *Rookes,* have not received wholehearted support from the Irish judiciary (*Dillon v. Dunnes Stores Ltd* (1968) and *McDonald v. Galvin* (1976)). In *Conway v. Irish National Teachers Organisation* (1991), the plaintiff was an eight-year-old pupil in Drimoleague national school when a teacher's strike commenced. As a result of a directive issued by the defendant to its members, the plaintiff was deprived of schooling from August 1976 until February 1977.

The defendant's liability in conspiracy had already been established in a related case (*Crowley v. Ireland* (1980)) and the only issue for determination was the assessment of damages. In his judgment, Finlay C.J. (while avoiding a specific discussion of the *Rookes* categories), expressly recognised the usefulness of exemplary damages, stating:

> ... the Court could not be availing of powers as ample as the defence of the Constitution and of constitutional rights require unless, in the case of breach of those rights, it held itself entitled to avail of one of the most effective deterrent powers which a civil court has: the awarding of exemplary or punitive damages.

Both McCarthy J. and Griffin J. in their judgments expressly rejected the application of the first category laid down in *Rookes* as applying to the case before them, with Griffin J. stating that he could see no valid reason why the award of such damages should be limited to situations where the oppressive or unconstitutional actions were the result of the actions of the government.

The courts will award exemplary damages only in the most exceptional of cases. Following the decision in *Conway,* judicial discretion to award such damages, particularly in non-constitutional tort actions, remains ambiguous. However, where it is deemed that a particular case gives rise to an award of such damages, it is clear that the courts must adhere to certain guidelines. Lord Devlin considered that the following factors should be taken into consideration by the court in making such a determination: (i) the plaintiff must be the victim of the punishable behaviour; (ii) the courts should exercise restraint since the award of exemplary damages equally may work against liberty; and (iii) the means of both plaintiff and defendant are material considerations in the court's determination. In *McIntyre v. Lewis* (1991), the Irish courts expressly approved of these guidelines, O'Flaherty J. expressing the view that the award of exemplary damages should be kept "on a tight rein."

The issue of exemplary damages poses complex problems for the judiciary in Ireland. The exact scope for the making of such awards remains unclear. In cases involving an infringement of constitutional rights, the Irish Supreme Court (*Conway*) has expressly rejected the categories laid down by Lord Devlin. The position regarding non-constitutional tort actions remains unsettled. McMahon & Binchy (2000, p.1135) express the view that any attempt to apply the *Rookes* limitations to such tort actions would be "futile [as] ... to do so would force plaintiffs to recharacterise traditional tort claims in constitutional terms ..."

The Irish Law Reform Commission examined this area in its *Report on Aggravated, Exemplary and Restitutionary Damages* (2000)). The Commission considered whether the award of exemplary damages should be confined, by means of legislation, to actions for defamation and those involving constitutional torts (para 1.58). This proposal did not recommend itself to the Commission, which was of the view that such an approach would, *inter alia*, unfairly single out defendants in a defamation action and would lead to a "constitutionalisation" of the law of torts. On the issue of when such damages should be awarded, the Report made the following recommendation (para.1.62):

> ... exemplary damages should be awarded only where compensatory and aggravated damages have an insufficient punitive and deterrent effect, and where there has been exceptional misconduct on the part of the defendant. However, given this context, we do not advocate restricting the scope of exemplary damages as regards the causes of action for which they may be awarded. We consider that restricting exemplary damages according to the quality of the defendant's mis-conduct would limit them to cases where compensatory damages would be an insufficient deterrent, and would also require moderation in the quantum of exemplary damages. These methods of restriction are more principled and less arbitrary than a restriction of exemplary damages based on the cause of action.

The Irish case law reflects the ambiguities that are present in this area and evidences a pressing need for judicial intervention as recom-mended by the Law Reform Commission. It is submitted that an approach whereby awards of exemplary damages are made based on "the quality of the defendant's misconduct" and not "based on the cause of action" (as outlined by the L.R.C.) would be the most appro-priate method by which this clarification could be achieved.

Further reading

McMahon & Binchy, *Law of Torts* (Butterworths, 2000), pp. 1119–1186; Quill, *Torts in Ireland* (Gill & Macmillian, 1999), pp. 470–497; Fleming, *The Law of Torts* (LBC, 1998), pp. 255–287; Weir, *A Case-book on Tort* (Sweet & Maxwell, 2000), pp. 635–359; Law Reform Commission, *Report on Aggravated, Exemplary and Restitutionary Damages* (LRC 60 – 2000); Healy, "Recent Developments in the Law of Damages" (November 2000) 6 *The Bar Review* 69; *Section 2 of the Civil Liability (Amendment) Act, 1964: The Deductability of Collateral Benefits from Awards of Damages* (Law Reform Commission Consul-tation Paper No. CP15-1999).

APPENDIX A

DEFAMATION ACT 1961

(No. 40 of 1961)

SELECTED PROVISIONS

1.—This Act may be cited as the Defamation Act, 1961.

PART III

CIVIL PROCEEDINGS FOR DEFAMATION

Interpretation (Part III)

14.—(1) In this Part—

"broadcast" has the same meaning as in the Wireless Telegraphy Act, 1926 (in this section referred to as the Act of 1926) and "broadcasting" shall be construed accordingly;

"broadcasting station" has the same meaning as in the Act of 1926, as amended by the Broadcasting Authority Act, 1960;

"wireless" telegraphy has the same meaning as in the Act of 1926.

(2) Any reference in this Part to words shall be construed as including a reference to visual images, gestures and other methods of signifying meaning.

(3) Where words broadcast by means of wireless telegraphy are simultaneously transmitted by telegraph as defined by the Telegraph Act, 1863, in accordance with a licence granted by the Minister for Posts and Telegraphs, the provisions of this Part shall apply as if the transmission were broadcasting by means of wireless telegraphy.

Broadcast statements

15.—For the purposes of the law of libel and slander the broadcasting of words by means of wireless telegraphy shall be treated as publication in permanent form.

Words imputing unchastity or adultery actionable without special damage

16.—Words spoken and published which impute unchastity or adultery to any woman or girl shall not require special damage to render them actionable.

Offer of an apology admissible in evidence in mitigation of damages in action for defamation

17.—In any action for defamation, it shall be lawful for the defendant (after notice in writing of his intention so to do, duly given to the plaintiff at the time of filing or delivering the plea in the action) to give in evidence, in mitigation of damage, that he made or offered an apology to the plaintiff for such defamation before the commencement of the action, or as soon as afterwards as he had an opportunity of doing so, in case the action shall have been commenced before there was an opportunity of making or of offering such apology.

Newspaper and broadcast reports of proceedings in court privileged

18.—(1) A fair and accurate report published in any newspaper or broadcast by means of wireless telegraphy as part of any programme or service provided by means of a broadcasting station within the State or in Northern Ireland of proceedings publicly heard before any court established by law and exercising judicial authority within the State or in Northern Ireland shall, if published or broadcast contemporaneously with such proceedings, be privileged.

(2) Nothing in subsection (1) of this section shall authorise the publication or broadcasting of any blasphemous or obscene matter.

Slander affecting official, professional or business reputation

19.—In an action for slander in respect of words calculated to disparage the plaintiff in any office, profession, calling, trade or business held or carried on by him at the time of the publication, but shall not be necessary to allege or prove special damage, whether or not the words are spoken of the plaintiff in the way of his office, profession, calling, trade or business.

Slander of title, etc.

20.—(1) In an action for slander of title, slander of goods or other malicious falsehood, it shall not be necessary to allege or prove special damage—

(a) if the words upon which the action is founded are calculated to cause pecuniary damage to the plaintiff and are published in writing or other permanent form; or

(b) if the said words calculated to cause pecuniary damage to the plaintiff in respect of any office, profession, calling, trade or business held or carried on by him at the time of the publication.

(2) Section 15 of this Act shall apply for the purposes of subsection (1) of this section as it applies for the purposes of the law of libel and slander.

Unintentional defamation

21.—(1) A person who has published words alleged to be defamatory of another person may, if he claims that the words were published by him innocently in relation to that other person, make an offer of amends under this section, and in any such case—

(a) if the offer is accepted by the party aggrieved and is duly performed, no proceedings for libel or slander shall be taken or continued by that party against the person making the offer in respect of the publication in question (but without prejudice to any cause of action against any other person jointly responsible for that publication);

(b)   if the offer is not accepted by the party aggrieved, then, except as
      otherwise provided by this section, it shall be a defence, in any
      proceedings by him for libel or slander against the person making
      the offer in respect of the publication in question, to prove that the
      words complained of were published by the defendant innocently
      in relation to the plaintiff and that the offer was made as soon as
      practicable after the defendant received notice that they were or
      might be defamatory of the plaintiff, and has not been withdrawn.

(2) An offer of amends under this section must be expressed to be
made for the purposes of this section, and must be accompanied by an
affidavit specifying the facts relied upon by the person making it to
show that the words in question were published by him innocently in
relation to the party aggrieved; and for the purposes of a defence under
paragraph (b) of subsection (1) of this section no evidence, other than
evidence of facts specified in the affidavit, shall be admissible on
behalf of that person to prove that the words were so published.

(3) An offer of amends under this section shall be understood to
mean an offer—

(a)   in any case, to publish or join in the publication of a suitable cor-
      rection of the words complained of, and a sufficient apology to
      the party aggrieved in respect of those words;

(b)   where copies of a document or record containing the said words
      have been distributed by or with the knowledge of the person
      making the offer, to take such steps as are reasonably practicable
      on his part for notifying persons to whom copies have been so
      distributed that the words are alleged to be defamatory of the
      party aggrieved.

(4) Where an offer of amends under this section is accepted by the
party aggrieved—

(a)   any question as to the steps to be taken in fulfilment of the offer
      as so accepted shall, in default of agreement between the parties,
      be referred to and determined by the High Court or, if proceed-
      ings in respect of the publication in question have been taken in
      the Circuit Court, by the Circuit Court, and the decision of such
      Court thereon shall be final;

(b)   the power of the court to make orders as to costs in proceedings
      by the party aggrieved against the person making the offer in
      respect of the publication in question, or in proceedings in respect

of the offer under paragraph (a) of this subsection, shall include power to order the payment by the person making the offer to the party aggrieved of costs on an indemnity basis and any expenses reasonably incurred or to be incurred by that party in consequence of the publication in question;

and if no such proceedings as aforesaid are taken, the High Court may, upon application made by the party aggrieved, make any such order for the payment of such costs and expenses as aforesaid as could be made in such proceedings.

(5) For the purposes of this section words shall be treated as published by one person (in this subsection referred to as the publisher) innocently in relation to another person if, and only if, the following conditions are satisfied, that is to say—

(a)   that the publisher did not intend to publish them of and concerning that other person, and did not know of circumstances by virtue of which they might be understood to refer to him; or

(b)   that the words were not defamatory on the face of them, and the publisher did not know of circumstances by virtue of which they might be understood to be defamatory of that other person,

and in either case that the publisher exercised all reasonable in relation to the publication; and any reference in this subsection to the publisher shall be construed as including a reference to any servant or agent of the publisher who was concerned with the contents of the publication—

(6) Paragraph (b) of subsection (1) of this section shall not apply where the party aggrieved proves that he has suffered special damage.

(7) Paragraph (b) of subsection (1) of this section shall not apply in relation to the publication by any person of words of which he is not the author unless he proves that the words were written by the author without malice.

Justification

22.—In an action for libel or slander in respect of words containing two or more distinct charges against the plaintiff, a defence of justification shall not fail by reason only that the truth of every charge is not proved, if the words not proved to be true do not materially injure the plaintiff's reputation having regard to the truth of the remaining charges.

Fair comment

23.—In an action for libel or slander in respect of words consisting partly of allegations of fact and partly of expression of opinion, a defence of fair comment shall not fail by reason only that the truth of every allegation of fact is not proved, if the expression of opinion is fair comment having regard to such of the facts alleged or referred to in the words complained of as are proved.

Qualified privilege of certain newspaper and broadcasting reports

24.—(1) Subject to the provisions of this section, the publication in a newspaper or the broadcasting by means of wireless telegraphy as part of any programme or service provided by means of a broadcasting station within the State or in Northern Ireland of any such report or other matter as is mentioned in the Second Schedule to this Act shall be privileged unless the publication or broadcasting is proved to be made with malice.

(2) In an action for libel in respect of the publication or broadcasting of any such report or matter as is mentioned in Part II of the Second Schedule to this Act, the provisions of this section shall not be a defence if it is proved that the defendant has been requested by the plaintiff to publish in the newspaper in which the original publication was made or to broadcast from the broadcasting station from which the original broadcast was made, whichever is the case, a reasonable statement by way of explanation or contradiction, and has refused or neglected to do so, or has done so in a manner not adequate or not reasonable having regard to all the circumstances.

(3) Nothing in this section shall be construed as protecting the publication or broadcasting of any matter the publication or broadcasting of which is prohibited by law, or of any matter which is not of public concern and the publication or broadcast of which is not for the public benefit.

(4) Nothing in this section shall be construed as limiting or bridging any privilege subsisting (otherwise than by virtue of section 4 of the Law of Libel Amendment Act, 1888) immediately before the commencement of this Act.

Agreements for indemnity

25.—An agreement for indemnifying any person against civil ability for libel in respect of the publication of any matter shall not be unlawful unless at the time of the publication that person knows that the matter is defamatory, and does not reasonably believe there is a good defence to any action brought upon it.

Evidence of other damages recovered by plaintiff

26.—In any action for libel or slander the defendant may give evidence in mitigation of damages that the plaintiff has recovered damages, or has brought actions for damages, for libel or slander n respect of the publication of words to the same effect as the words on which the action is founded, or has received or agreed to receive compensation in respect of any such publication.

Obligation on certain newspaper proprietors to be registered under the Registration of Business Names Act, 1916

27.—(1) The proprietor of every newspaper having a place of business in the State shall, where such proprietor is not a company registered under the Companies Acts, 1908 to 1959, and is not required under the provisions of the Registration of Business Names Act, 1916, to be registered under that Act in respect of the business of carrying on such newspaper, be registered in the manner directed by that Act, and that Act shall apply to such proprietor in like manner as it applies to a film or individual referred to in section 1 thereof.

(2) Every reference in the Registration of Business Names Act, 1916, to that Act shall be construed as a reference to that Act as extended by subsection (1) of this section.

(3) In this section "newspaper" means any paper containing public news or observations thereon, or consisting wholly or mainly of advertisements, which is printed for sale and is published in the State either periodically or in parts or numbers at intervals not exceeding twenty-six days.

Saving

28.—Nothing in this Part shall affect the law relating to criminal libel.

APPENDIX B

OCCUPIERS' LIABILITY ACT 1995

(No. 10 of 1995)

AN ACT TO AMEND THE LAW RELATING TO THE LIABILITY OF OCCUPIERS OF PREMISES (INCLUDING LAND) IN RESPECT OF DANGERS EXISTING ON SUCH PREMISES FOR INJURY OR DAMAGE TO PERSONS OR PROPERTY WHILE ON SUCH PREMISES AND TO PROVIDE FOR CONNECTED MATTERS.

[17th June, 1995]

BE IT ENACTED BY THE OIREACHTAS AS FOLLOWS:

Interpretation

1.—(1) In this Act, unless the context otherwise requires—

"damage" includes loss of property and injury to an animal;

"danger", in relation to any premises, means a danger due to the state of the premises;

"entrant", in relation to a danger existing on premises, means a person who enters on the premises and is not the sole occupier;

"injury" includes loss of life, any disease and any impairment of physical or mental condition;

"occupier", in relation to any premises, means a person exercising such control over the state of the premises that it is reasonable to impose upon that person a duty towards an entrant in respect of a particular danger thereon and, where there is more than one occupier of the same premises, the extent of the duty of each occupier towards an entrant depends on the degree of control each of them has over the state of the premises and the particular danger thereon and whether, as respects each of them, the entrant concerned is a visitor, recreational user or trespasser;

"premises" includes land, water and any fixed or moveable structures thereon and also includes vessels, vehicles, trains, aircraft and other means of transport;

"property", in relation to an entrant, includes the property of another in the possession or under the control of the entrant while the entrant is on the premises of the occupier;

"recreational activity" means any recreational activity conducted, whether alone or with others, in the open air (including any sporting activity), scientific research and nature study so conducted, exploring caves and visiting sites and buildings of historical, architectural, traditional, artistic, archaeological or scientific importance;

"recreational user" means an entrant who, with or without the occupier's permission or at the occupier's implied invitation, is present on premises without a charge (other than a reasonable charge in respect of the cost of providing vehicle parking facilities) being imposed for the purpose of engaging in a recreational activity, including an entrant admitted without charge to a national monument pursuant to section 16 (1) of the National Monuments Act, 1930, but not including an entrant who is so present and is—

(a) a member of the occupier's family who is ordinarily resident on the premises,

(b) an entrant who is present at the express invitation of the occupier or such a member, or

(c) an entrant who is present with the permission of the occupier or such a member for social reasons connected with the occupier or such a member;

"trespasser" means an entrant other than a recreational user or visitor;

"visitor" means—

(a) an entrant, other than a recreational user, who is present on premises at the invitation, or with the permission, of the occupier or any other entrant specified in paragraph (a), (b) or (c) of the definition of "recreational user",

(b) an entrant, other than a recreational user, who is present on premises by virtue of an express or implied term in a contract, and

(c) an entrant as of right,

while he or she is so present, as the case may be, for the purpose for which he or she is invited or permitted to be there, for the purpose of the performance of the contract or for the purpose of the exercise of the right, and includes any such entrant whose presence on premises has become unlawful after entry thereon and who is taking reasonable steps to leave.

(2) In this Act—

(a) a reference to a section is to a section of this Act, unless it is indicated that reference to some other enactment is intended,

(b) a reference to a subsection is to the subsection of the provision in which the reference occurs, unless it is indicated that reference to some other provision is intended, and

(c) a reference to any enactment shall be construed as a reference to that enactment as amended, adapted or extended by or under any subsequent enactment including this Act.

Replacement of common law rules

2.—(1) Subject to section 8, the duties, liabilities and rights provided for by this Act shall have effect in place of the duties, liabilities and rights which heretofore attached by the common law to occupiers of premises as such in respect of dangers existing on their premises to entrants thereon.

(2) This Act does not apply to a cause of action which accrued before the commencement of this Act.

Duty owed to visitors

3.—(1) An occupier of premises owes a duty of care ("the common duty of care") towards a visitor thereto except in so far as the occupier extends, restricts, modifies or excludes that duty in accordance with section 5.

(2) In this section "the common duty of care" means a duty to take such care as is reasonable in all the circumstances (having regard to the care which a visitor may reasonably be expected to take for his or her own safety and, if the visitor is on the premises in the company of another person, the extent of the supervision and control the latter person may reasonably be expected to exercise over the visitor's activities)

to ensure that a visitor to the premises does not suffer injury or damage by reason of any danger existing thereon.

Duty owed to recreational users or trespassers

4.—(1) In respect of a danger existing on premises, an occupier owes towards a recreational user of the premises or a trespasser thereon ("the person") a duty—

(a) not to injure the person or damage the property of the person intentionally, and

(b) not to act with reckless disregard for the person or the property of the person,

except in so far as the occupier extends the duty in accordance with section 5.

(2) In determining whether or not an occupier has so acted with reckless disregard, regard shall be had to all the circumstances of the case, including—

(a) whether the occupier knew or had reasonable grounds for believing that a danger existed on the premises;

(b) whether the occupier knew or had reasonable grounds for believing that the person and, in the case of damage, property of the person, was or was likely to be on the premises;

(c) whether the occupier knew or had reasonable grounds for believing that the person or property of the person was in, or was likely to be in, the vicinity of the place where the danger existed;

(d) whether the danger was one against which, in all the circumstances, the occupier might reasonably be expected to provide protection for the person and property of the person;

(e) the burden on the occupier of eliminating the danger or of protecting the person and property of the person from the danger, taking into account the difficulty, expense or impracticability, having regard to the character of the premises and the degree of the danger, of so doing;

(f) the character of the premises including, in relation to premises of such a character as to be likely to be used for recreational activity, the desirability of maintaining the tradition of open access to premises of such a character for such an activity;

(g) the conduct of the person, and the care which he or she may reasonably be expected to take for his or her own safety, while on the premises, having regard to the extent of his or her knowledge thereof;

(h) the nature of any warning given by the occupier or another person of the danger; and

(i) whether or not the person was on the premises in the company of another person and, if so, the extent of the supervision and control the latter person might reasonably be expected to exercise over the other's activities.

(3) (a) Where a person enters onto premises for the purpose of committing an offence or, while present thereon, commits an offence, the occupier shall not be liable for a breach of the duty imposed by subsection (1) (b) unless a court determines otherwise in the interests of justice.

(b) In paragraph (a) "offence" includes an attempted offence.

(4) Notwithstanding subsection (1), where a structure on premises is or has been provided for use primarily by recreational users, the occupier shall owe a duty towards such users in respect of such a structure to take reasonable care to maintain the structure in a safe condition:
Provided that, where a stile, gate, footbridge or other similar structure on premises is or has been provided not for use primarily by recreational users, the occupier's duty towards a recreational user thereof in respect of such structure shall not be extended by virtue of this subsection.

Modification of occupiers' duty to entrants

5.—(1) An occupier may by express agreement or notice extend his or her duty towards entrants under sections 3 and 4.

(2) (a) Subject to this section and to section 8, an occupier may by express agreement or notice restrict, modify or exclude his or her duty towards visitors under section 3.

(b) Such a restriction, modification or exclusion shall not bind a visitor unless—

   (i) it is reasonable in all the circumstances, and

   (ii) in case the occupier purports by notice to so restrict, modify or exclude that duty, the occupier has taken reasonable steps to bring the notice to the attention of the visitor.

(c) For the purposes of paragraph (b) (ii) an occupier shall be presumed, unless the contrary is shown, to have taken reasonable steps to bring a notice to the attention of a visitor if it is prominently displayed at the normal means of access to the premises.

(3) In respect of a danger existing on premises, a restriction, modification or exclusion referred to in subsection (2) shall not be taken as allowing an occupier to injure a visitor or damage the property of a visitor intentionally or to act with reckless disregard for a visitor or the property of a visitor.

(4) In determining for the purposes of subsection (3) whether or not an occupier has acted with reckless disregard, regard shall be had to all the circumstances of the case including, where appropriate, the matters specified in subsection (2) of section 4.

(5) Where injury or damage is caused to a visitor or property of a visitor by a danger of which the visitor had been warned by the occupier or another person, the warning is not, without more, to be treated as absolving the occupier from liability unless, in all the circumstances, it was enough to enable the visitor, by having regard to the warning, to avoid the injury or damage so caused.

Duty of occupiers towards strangers to contracts

6.—(1) The duty which an occupier of premises owes to an entrant under this Act shall not be capable of being modified or excluded by a contract to which the entrant is a stranger, whether the occupier is bound by the contract to permit the entrant to enter or use the premises or not.

(2) For the purposes of this section, an entrant shall be deemed to be a stranger to a contract if the entrant is not for the time being entitled to the benefit of the contract as a party to it or as the successor by assignment or otherwise of a party to it, and, accordingly, a party to the contract who has ceased to be so entitled shall be deemed to be a stranger to the contract.

(3) This section applies to contracts entered into before the commencement of this Act, as well as to those entered into after such commencement.

Liability of occupiers for negligence of independent contractors

7.—An occupier of premises shall not be liable to an entrant for injury or damage caused to the entrant or property of the entrant by reason of a danger existing on the premises due to the negligence of an independent contractor employed by the occupier if the occupier has taken all reasonable care in the circumstances (including such steps as the occupier ought reasonably to have taken to satisfy himself or herself that the independent contractor was competent to do the work concerned) unless the occupier has or ought to have had knowledge of the fact that the work was not properly done.

Saver

8.—Nothing in this Act shall be construed as affecting any enactment or any rule of law relating to—

(a) self-defence, the defence of others or the defence of property,

(b) any liability imposed on an occupier as a member of a particular class of persons including the following classes of persons:

(i) persons by virtue of a contract for the hire of, or for the carriage for reward of persons or property in, any vessel, vehicle, train, aircraft or other means of transport;

(ii) persons by virtue of a contract of bailment; and

(iii) employers in respect of their duties towards their employees, or

(c) any liability imposed on an occupier for a tort committed by another person in circumstances where the duty imposed on the occupier is of such a nature that its performance may not be delegated to another person.

Short title and commencement

9.—(1) This Act may be cited as the Occupiers' Liability Act, 1995.

(2) This Act shall come into operation one month after the date of its passing.

ACT REFERRED TO

National Monuments Act, 1930   1930, No. 2

APPENDIX C

LIABILITY FOR DEFECTIVE PRODUCTS ACT 1991

(No. 28 of 1991)

AN ACT TO ENABLE EFFECT TO BE GIVEN TO THE PROVISIONS OF DIRECTIVE NO. 85/374/EEC OF 25 JULY 1985 OF THE COUNCIL OF THE EUROPEAN COMMUNITIES ON THE APPROXIMATION OF THE LAWS, REGULATIONS AND ADMINISTRATIVE PROVISIONS OF THE MEMBER STATES OF THE EUROPEAN COMMUNITIES CONCERNING LIABILITY FOR DEFECTIVE PRODUCTS.

[4th December, 1991]

BE IT ENACTED BY THE OIREACHTAS AS FOLLOWS:

Interpretation

1.—(1) In this Act, except where the context otherwise requires—

"the Council Directive" means Council Directive No. 85/374/EEC of 25 July 1985 (O.J. No. L210 of 7.8.1985, p.29) the text of which in the English language is set out for convenience of reference in the Schedule to this Act;

"damage" means—

(a) death or personal injury, or

(b) loss of, damage to, or destruction of, any item of property other than the defective product itself:

Provided that the item of property—

(i) is of a type ordinarily intended for private use or consumption, and

(ii) was used by the injured person mainly for his own private use or consumption;

"initial processing" means, in relation to primary agricultural products, any processing of an industrial nature of those products which could cause a defect therein;

"injured person" means a person who has suffered damage caused wholly or partly by a defect in a product or, if he has died, his personal representative (within the meaning of section 3 of the Succession Act, 1965) or dependants (within the meaning of section 47 (1) of the Civil Liability Act, 1961);

"Member State" means a Member State of the European Communities;

"the Minister" means the Minister for Industry and Commerce;

"personal injury" includes any disease and any impairment of a person's physical or mental condition;

"primary agricultural products" means the products of the soil, of stock-farming and of fisheries and game, excluding such products and game which have undergone initial processing;

"producer" shall be construed in accordance with section 2 of this Act;

"product" means all movables with the exception of primary agricultural products which have not undergone initial processing, and includes—

(a) movables even though incorporated into another product or into an immovable, whether by virtue of being a component part or raw material or otherwise,

(b) electricity where damage is caused as a result of a failure in the process of generation of electricity.

(2) A word or expression that is used in this Act and is also used in the Council Directive has, unless the contrary intention appears, the meaning in this Act that it has in the Council Directive.

(3) In construing a provision of this Act, a court shall give it a construction that will give effect to the Council Directive, and for this purpose a court shall have regard to the provisions of the Council Directive, including its preamble.

(4) In this Act a reference to any other enactment shall be construed as a reference to that enactment as amended by or under any other enactment, including this Act.

Liability for damage caused by defective products

2.—(1) The producer shall be liable in damages in tort for damage caused wholly or partly by a defect in his product.

(2) In this Act, "producer" means—

   (a) the manufacturer or producer of a finished product, or

   (b) the manufacturer or producer of any raw material or the manufacturer or producer of a component part of a product, or

   (c) in the case of the products of the soil, of stock-farming and of fisheries and game, which have undergone initial processing, the person who carried out such processing, or

   (d) any person who, by putting his name, trade mark or other distinguishing feature on the product or using his name or any such mark or feature in relation to the product, has held himself out to be the producer of the product, or

   (e) any person who has imported the product into a Member State from a place outside the European Communities in order, in the course of any business of his, to supply it to another, or

   (f) any person who is liable as producer of the product pursuant to subsection (3) of this section.

(3) Without prejudice to subsection (1) of this section, where damage is caused wholly or partly by a defect in a product, any person who supplied the product (whether to the person who suffered the damage, to the producer of any product in which the product is comprised or to any other person) shall, where the producer of the product cannot by taking reasonable steps be identified, be liable, as the producer, for the damage if—

   (a) the injured person requests the supplier to identify any person (whether still in existence or not) to whom paragraph (a), (b), (c), (d) or (e) of subsection (2) of this section applies in relation to the product,

   (b) that request is made within a reasonable time after the damage occurs and at a time when it is not reasonably practicable for the injured person to identify all those persons, and

(c) the supplier fails, within a reasonable time after receiving the request, either to comply with the request or to identify the person who supplied the product to him.

Limitation of damages

3.—(1) Where, but for this section, damages not exceeding £350 in respect of loss of or damage to, or destruction of, any item of property other than the defective product itself would fall to be awarded by virtue of this Act, no damages shall be awarded, and where, but for this section, damages exceeding that amount would fall to be awarded, only that excess shall be awarded.

(2) The Minister may by order vary with effect from a date specified in the order, being a date subsequent to the making of the order, the amount specified in subsection (1) of this section but such variation shall not apply to proceedings pending in any court at that date.

(3) The Minister may by order amend or revoke an order made under this section.

Proof of damage and defect

4.—The onus shall be on the injured person concerned to prove the damage, the defect and the causal relationship between the defect and damage.

Defective product

5.—(1) For the purposes of this Act a product is defective if it fails to provide the safety which a person is entitled to expect, taking all circumstances into account, including—

(a) the presentation of the product,

(b) the use to which it could reasonably be expected that the product would be put, and

(c) the time when the product was put into circulation.

(2) A product shall not be considered defective for the sole reason that a better product is subsequently put into circulation.

Defences

6.—A producer shall not be liable under this Act if he proves—

(a) that he did not put the product into circulation, or

(b) that, having regard to the circumstances, it is probable that the defect which caused the damage did not exist at the time when the product was put into circulation by him or that that defect came into being afterwards, or

(c) that the product was neither manufactured by him for sale or any form of distribution for an economic purpose nor manufactured or distributed by him in the course of his business, or

(d) that the defect concerned is due to compliance by the product with any requirement imposed by or under any enactment or any requirement of the law of the European Communities, or

(e) that the state of scientific and technical knowledge at the time when he put the product into circulation was not such as to enable the existence of the defect to be discovered, or

(f) in the case of the manufacturer of a component or the producer of a raw material, that the defect is attributable entirely to the design of the product in which the component has been fitted or the raw material has been incorporated or to the instructions given by the manufacturer of the product.

Limitation of actions

7.—(1) An action for the recovery of damages under this Act shall not be brought after the expiration of three years from the date on which the cause of action accrued or the date (if later) on which the plaintiff became aware, or should reasonably have become aware, of the damage, the defect and the identity of the producer.

(2) (a) A right of action under this Act shall be extinguished upon the expiration of the period of ten years from the date on which the producer put into circulation the actual product which caused the damage unless the injured person has in the meantime instituted proceedings against the producer.

(b) Paragraph (a) of this subsection shall have effect whether or not the right of action accrued or time began to run during the period referred to in subsection (1) of this section.

(3) Sections 9 of the Civil Liability Act, 1961, shall not apply to an action for the recovery of damages under this Act.

(4) The Statutes of Limitation, 1957 and 1991, shall apply to an action under this Act subject to the provisions of this section.

(5) For the purposes of subsection (4)—

(a) subsection (1) of this section shall be deemed to be a provision of the Statute of Limitations (Amendment) Act, 1991, of the kind referred to in section 2 (1) of that Act,

(b) "injury" where it occurs in that Act except in section 2 (1) (b) thereof includes damage to property, and "person injured" and "injured" shall be construed accordingly, and

(c) the reference in subsection (1) of this section to the date when the plaintiff became aware, or should reasonably have become aware, of the damage, the defect and the identity of the producer shall be construed in accordance with section 2 of that Act, but nothing in this paragraph shall prejudice the application of section 1 (3) of this Act.

Joint and several liability

8.—Where two or more persons are liable by virtue of this Act for the same damage, they shall be liable jointly and severally as concurrent wrongdoers within the meaning of Part III of the Civil Liability Act, 1961.

Reduction of liability

9.—(1) Without prejudice to Part III of the Civil Liability Act, 1961, concerning the right of contribution, the liability of the producer shall not be reduced when damage is caused both by a defect in a product and by the act or omission of a third party.

(2) Where any damage is caused partly by a defect in a product and partly by the fault of the injured person or of any person for whom the injured person is responsible, the provisions of the Civil Liability Act, 1961, concerning contributory negligence, shall have effect as if the

defect were due to the fault of every person liable by virtue of this Act for the damage caused by the defect.

Prohibition on exclusion from liability

10.—The liability of a producer arising by virtue of this Act to an injured person shall not be limited or excluded by any term of contract, by any notice or by any other provision.

Other rights of action not precluded

11.—This Act shall not affect any rights which an injured person may have under any enactment or under any rule of law.

Application of Courts Act, 1988

12.—Section 1 of the Courts Act, 1988, shall apply to an action in the High Court claiming damages under this Act or a question of fact or an issue arising in such an action as if such damages were mentioned in subsection (1) (a) of that section.

Application of this Act

13.—This Act shall not apply to any product put into circulation within the territory of any Member State before the commencement of this Act.

Short title and commencement

14.—(1) This Act may be cited as the Liability for Defective Products Act, 1991.

(2) This Act shall come into operation on such day as the Minister may appoint by order.

Section 1

SCHEDULE

Omitted.

APPENDIX D1

STATUE OF LIMITATIONS 1957

(No. 6 of 1957)

SELECTED PROVISIONS

Limitation of actions of contract and tort and certain other actions

11.(2)(a) Subject to paragraphs (b) and (c) of this subsection, an action founded on tort shall not be brought after the expiration of six years from the date on which the cause of action accrued.

(b) An action claiming damages for negligence, nuisance or breach of duty (whether the duty exists by virtue of a contract or of a provision made by or under a statute or independently of any contract or any such provision), where the damages claimed by the plaintiff for the negligence, nuisance or breach of duty consist of or include damages in respect of personal injuries to any person, shall not be brought after the expiration of three years from the date on which the cause of action accrued.

(c) An action claiming damages for slander shall not be brought after the expiration of three years from the date on which the cause of action accrued.

Extension of limitation period in case of disability

49.(1)(a) If, on the date when any right of action accrued for which a period of limitation is fixed by this Act, the person to whom it accrued was under a disability, the action may, subject to the subsequent provisions of this section, be brought at any time before the expiration of six years from the date when the person ceased to be under a disability or died, whichever event first occurred notwithstanding that the period of limitation has expired.

(b) Paragraph (a) of this subsection shall not affect any case where the right of action first accrued to some person (not under a disability) through whom the person under a disability claims.

(c) Where a right of action which has accrued to a person under a disability accrues, on the death of that person while still under a disability, to another person under a disability, no further extension of time shall be allowed by reason of the disability of the second person.

(d) None of the following actions—

   (i)   an action to recover land or money charged on land,

   (ii) an action by an incumbrancer claiming sale of land,

   (iii) an action in respect of a right in the nature of a lien for money's worth in or over land for a limited period not exceeding life, such as a right of support or a right of residence, not being an exclusive right of residence in or on a specified part of the land,

   shall be brought by virtue of paragraph (a) of this subsection by any person after the expiration of thirty years from the date on which the right of action accrued to that person or to some person through whom he claims.

(e) This section shall not apply to an action to recover a penalty or forfeiture, or a sum by way of penalty or forfeiture, recoverable by virtue of any enactment, except where the action is brought by the party grieved.

Postponement of limitation period in case of fraud

71. (1) Where, in the case of an action for which a period of limitation is fixed by this Act, either—

(a) the action is based on the fraud of the defendant or his agent or of any person through whom he claims or his agent, or

(b) the right of action is concealed by the fraud of any such person, the period of limitation shall not begin to run until the plaintiff has discovered the fraud or could with reasonable diligence have discovered it.

(2) Nothing in subsection (1) of this section shall enable an action to be brought to recover, or enforce any charge against, or set aside any transaction affecting any property which has been purchased for valuable consideration by a person who was not a party to the fraud and did not at the time of the purchase know or have reason to believe that any fraud had been committed.

Postponement of limitation period in case of mistake

72. (1) Where, in the case of any action for which a period of limitation is fixed by this Act, the action is for relief from the consequences of mistake, the period of limitation shall not begin to run until the plaintiff has discovered the mistake or could with reasonable diligence have discovered it.

(2) Nothing in subsection (1) of this section shall enable any action to be brought to recover, or enforce any charge against, or set aside any transaction affecting, any property which has been purchased for valuable consideration, subsequently to the transaction in which the mistake was made, by a person who did not know or have reason to believe that the mistake was made.

APPENDIX D2

STATUE OF LIMITATIONS (AMENDMENT) ACT 1991

(No. 18 of 1991)

Definition

1.—In this Act "the Principal Act" means the Statute of Limitations, 1957.

Date of knowledge for the purposes of this Act

2.—(1) For the purposes of any provision of this Act whereby the time within which an action in respect of an injury may be brought depends on a person's date of knowledge (whether he is the person injured or a personal representative or dependant of the person injured) references to that person's date of knowledge are references to the date on which he first had knowledge of the following facts:

- (a) that the person alleged to have been injured had been injured,
- (b) that the injury in question was significant,
- (c) that the injury was attributable in whole or in part to the act or omission which is alleged to constitute negligence, nuisance or breach of duty,
- (d) the identity of the defendant, and
- (e) if it is alleged that the act or omission was that of a person other than the defendant, the identity of that person and the additional facts supporting the bringing of an action against the defendant;

and knowledge that any acts or omissions did or did not, as a matter of law, involve negligence, nuisance or breach of duty is irrelevant.

(2) For the purposes of this section, a person's knowledge includes knowledge which he might reasonably have been expected to acquire—

- (a) from facts observable or ascertainable by him, or

(b) from facts ascertainable by him with the help of medical or other appropriate expert advice which it is reasonable for him to seek.

(3) Notwithstanding subsection (2) of this section—

(a) a person shall not be fixed under this section with knowledge of a fact ascertainable only with the help of expert advice so long as he has taken all reasonable steps to obtain (and, where appropriate, to act on) that advice; and

(b) a person injured shall not be fixed under this section with knowledge of a fact relevant to the injury which he has failed to acquire as a result of that injury.

Special time limit for actions in respect of personal injuries

3.—(1) An action, other than one to which section 6 of this Act applies, claiming damages in respect of personal injuries to a person caused by negligence, nuisance or breach of duty (whether the duty exists by virtue of a contract or of a provision made by or under a statute or independently of any contract or any such provision) shall not be brought after the expiration of three years from the date on which the cause of action accrued or the date of knowledge (if later) of the person injured.

(2) Section 11 (2) of the Principal Act is hereby amended by the substitution of the following paragraph for paragraphs (a) and (b):

"(a) Subject to paragraph (c) of this subsection and to section 3 (1) of the Statute of Limitations (Amendment) Act, 1991, an action founded on tort shall not be brought after the expiration of six years from the date on which the cause of action accrued.".

(3) Notwithstanding section 11 (2) (d) (inserted by section 13 (8) of the Sale of Goods and Supply of Services Act, 1980) of the Principal Act, an action for damages under section 13 (7) of the said Act of 1980 which consist of or include damages in respect of personal injuries to any person may be brought within two years of the date of knowledge of the person injured if that date is later than the date on which the cause of action accrued.

(4) The reference in section 21 (4) (b) of the Control of Dogs Act, 1986, to section 11 (2) (b) of the Principal Act shall be construed as a reference to subsection (1) of this section.

Survival of causes of action to which section 3 applies

4.—(1) If an injured person to whom section 3 of this Act applies dies before the expiration of the period specified in that section, any action that may be brought for the benefit of his estate in respect of a cause of action to which that section applies by virtue of section 7 of the Civil Liability Act, 1961, may be brought at any time before the expiration of three years from—

(a) the date of death, or

(b) the date of the personal representative's knowledge,

whichever is the later.

(2) For the purposes of this section—

(a) "personal representative" includes any person who is or has been a personal representative of the deceased, including an executor who has not proved the will (whether or not he has renounced probate), and

(b) where a person acquires knowledge of the injury before his appointment as personal representative of the deceased, the date of knowledge of that person shall be taken to be the date of his appointment as personal representative.

(3) If there is more than one personal representative and their dates of knowledge are different, subsection (1) (b) of this section shall be construed as referring to the earliest of those dates.

Extension of limitation period in case of disability

5.—(1) Notwithstanding anything in section 49 (1) (a) of the Principal Act, if, in the case of—

(a) an action of the kind to which section 3 of this Act applies, or

(b) an action under section 48 (1) of the Civil Liability Act, 1961 (being an action where death is caused by wrongful act, neglect or default), the person having the right to bring the action was under a disability either at the time when that right accrued to him or at the date of his knowledge, the action may be brought at any time before the expiration of three years from the date when he ceased to be under a disability or died, whichever event first occurred, notwithstanding that the period specified in the said section 3 has expired, but section 49 (1) (c) of the Principal Act shall apply accordingly.

(2) Subsection (1) of this section shall not affect any case where the right of action first accrued to some person (not under a disability) through whom the person under a disability claims.

(3) Notwithstanding section 49 (5) of the Principal Act (inserted by section 13 (8) of the Sale of Goods and Supply of Services Act, 1980), in the case of an action under section 13 (7) of the said Act of 1980, of the kind to which section 3 of this Act applies, subsections (1) and (2) of this section shall have effect as if for the words "three years" there were substituted the words "two years".

(4) Section 49 (2) of the Principal Act is hereby repealed.

Period of limitation in cases of fatal injuries

6.—(1) An action under section 48 (1) of the Civil Liability Act, 1961, shall not be brought after the expiration of three years from—

(a) the date of death, or

(b) the date of knowledge of the person for whose benefit the action is brought,

whichever is the later.

(2) Where there is more than one person for whose benefit an action under section 48 (1) of the Civil Liability Act, 1961, is brought, subsection (1) (b) of this section shall be applied separately to each of them.

(3) If, by virtue of subsection (2) of this section, the action would be outside the time limit applicable by virtue of subsection (1) of this section as regards one or more, but not all, of the persons for whose benefit it is brought, the court shall direct that any person as regards whom the action would be outside that limit shall be excluded from those for whom the action is brought.

(4) The court shall not give such a direction if it is shown that if the action were brought exclusively for the benefit of the person in question it would not be defeated by a defence of limitation, whether in

consequence of section 5 of this Act or of an agreement between the parties not to raise the defence or otherwise.

(5) Section 48 (6) of the Civil Liability Act, 1961, is hereby repealed.

Application of Act

7.—This Act shall apply to all causes of action whether accruing before or after its passing and to proceedings pending at its passing.

Short title, construction and collective citation

8.—(1) This Act may be cited as the Statute of Limitations (Amendment) Act, 1991.

(2) The Principal Act and this Act shall be construed as one, and may be cited together as the Statutes of Limitation, 1957 and 1991.

APPENDIX D3

STATUTE OF LIMITATIONS (AMENDMENT) ACT 2000

(No. 13 of 2000)

Short title, construction and collective citation

1.— (1) This Act may be cited as the Statute of Limitations (Amendment) Act, 2000.

(2) The Statutes of Limitation, 1957 and 1991, and this Act may be cited as the Statutes of Limitations and shall be construed together as one Act.

Amendment of Statute of Limitations, 1957

2.—The Statute of Limitations, 1957, is hereby amended by the insertion of the following section after section 48:

"Disability of certain persons for purpose of bringing certain actions arising out of acts of sexual abuse

48A.—(1) A person shall, for the purpose of bringing an action—

(a) founded on tort in respect of an act of sexual abuse committed against him or her at a time when he or she had not yet reached full age, or

(b) against a person (other than the person who committed that act), claiming damages for negligence or breach of duty where the damages claimed consist of or include damages in respect of personal injuries caused by such act,

be under a disability while he or she is suffering from any psychological injury that—

(i) is caused, in whole or in part, by that act, or any other act, of the person who committed the first-mentioned act, and

(ii) is of such significance that his or her will, or his or her ability to make a reasoned decision, to bring such action is substantially impaired.

(2) This section applies to actions referred to in subsection (1) whether the cause of action concerned accrued before or after the passing of the Statute of Limitations (Amendment) Act, 2000, including actions pending at such passing.

(3) An action referred to in subsection (1), that but for this subsection could not, by virtue of this Act, be brought, may be brought not later than one year after the passing of the Statute of Limitations (Amendment) Act, 2000, provided that, after the expiration of the period within which such action could by virtue of this Act have been brought, but prior to 30 March, 2000—

(a) the person bringing the action obtained professional legal advice that caused him or her to believe that the action could not, by virtue of this Act, be brought, or

(b) a complaint to the Garda Síochána was made by or on behalf of such person in respect of the act to which the action relates.

(4) Subsection (3) shall not apply to an action referred to in subsection (1) where final judgement has been given in respect of the action.

(5) This section is in addition to and not in substitution for section 48 of this Act.

(6) For the purposes of this section, a judgment shall be deemed to be a final judgment where—

(a) the time within which an appeal against the judgment may be brought has expired and no such appeal has been brought,

(b) there is no provision for an appeal from such judgment, or

(c) an appeal against the judgment has been withdrawn.

(7) In this section—
'an act of sexual abuse' includes—

(a) any act of causing, inducing or coercing a person to participate in any sexual activity,

(b) any act of causing, inducing or coercing the person to observe any other person engaging in any sexual activity, or

(c) any act committed against, or in the presence of, a person that
any reasonable person would, in all the circumstances, regard
as misconduct of a sexual nature:

Provided that the doing or commission of the act concerned is recognised by law as giving rise to a cause of action;

'full age' means—

(a) in relation to a person against whom an act of sexual abuse
was committed before the commencement of the Age   of
Majority Act, 1985, 21 years, and

(b) in relation to a person against whom an act of sexual abuse
was committed after such commencement, full age within the
meaning of that Act;

'professional legal advice' means advice given by a practising barrister
or solicitor in circumstances where the person to whom the advice was
given sought such advice for the purpose of bringing or prosecuting an
action to which subsection (1) applies, whether such an action was
brought or not.".

Saver in relation to court's power to dismiss on ground of delay

3.—Nothing in section 48A of the Statute of Limitations, 1957
(inserted by section 2 of this Act), shall be construed as affecting any
power of a court to dismiss an action on the ground of there being such
delay between the accrual of the cause of action and the bringing of the
action as, in the interests of justice, would warrant its dismissal.

INDEX